M
WORLDS

Joseph P. Hayes

Unrelenting Little Efforts

The Art of Achievement

europe books

© 2022 **Europe Books** | London
www.europebooks.co.uk – info@europebooks.co.uk

ISBN 9791220122856
First edition: May 2022

Unrelenting Little Efforts
The Art of Achievement

*To my wife Linda.
This book could not have been
written without her constant
corrections, editing, and most of all
her valuable suggestions.*

Introduction

Unrelenting Little Efforts, that's the only way I survived and succeeded in all the different careers I've had. I believe I was the ultimate job hopper. It is not a lifestyle I would recommend. I'm convinced that any person who stays on course with a single vocation will find that success grows naturally over time. I always thought the grass was greener, and I changed jobs frequently. Still, I achieved success, but I'm certain had I focused on one career, my triumphs would have been greater. Nevertheless, I did gain knowledge and experience you can only get by working in vastly different domains. One of the greatest skills I picked up was the ability to train people and help put them on the fast track to success. Now I've connected with you and I'm going to do everything in my power to give you the winning edge. I've discovered through my experience that a person can advance consistently and live the best life they can imagine.

This is not an autobiography, but I want you to know about some of my learning experiences, so you can profit from them. I want to pass on the knowledge and skills I've gained, to give you some advantages that I've enjoyed. Just for the record I spent 4 proud years in the Marine Corps, and then I began my quest for success working at the following occupations randomly listed below.

Disk Jockey
Radio Announcer
Opened and Operated Beach Front Hot Dog Stand

Data Center Computer Operator
Meat Cutter

Real Estate Broker
Started A Home Security Business
Computer Hardware Sales
Motivational Speaker
Applications Programmer
Computer Software Sales
Manager-Hi Tech Recruiting Firm
Vice President of a Construction Company
Computer Memory Sales
Telecommunications Coordinator
Systems Programmer
Project Manager

I actively worked into my seventh decade and currently I am a successful independent stock trader. My aim in this book is to convey what I've learned, to help other success seekers speed up their progress and go beyond the norm to exceptional success.

My biggest joy has been in training people. I didn't start out that way, and as far as I can recall I never sought a position where I would train people as a major part of my responsibility. I stumbled into it because my ability to teach was noticed by co-workers and managers. In many different careers training became part of my job description. I wanted to make the trainees feel comfortable, knowing my reassurance would boost confidence. I also encouraged them to outshine by striving to leave their mark of excellence on every task they were assigned. Now I'm on a bigger mission, I want to help all those reading this to find success. I could write an entire book on training others, instead I will leave you with a few examples of experiences that shaped my life.

In the Marine Corps, every year Marines are required to qualify for marksmanship on the rifle range. It's difficult, not everyone qualifies. There are three classifications, Marksman, Sharpshooter, and Expert. I qualified as an Expert with a very high score. This led to my being assigned to a special team with other high scoring Marines. Everyone on this team was in competition and looking to make good because there was the possibility of being selected for the U.S. Olympic tryouts. As a member of this select team, they issued me a special rifle, with a leather strap. I could not get comfortable with the new rifle and leather strap. I wished they had let me use my own standard issue rifle with a canvas strap. I was 19 years old and much younger than the other team members. I felt intimidated, even though I had a higher qualifying score than many others on the team. Feeling that I was out of my league, all confidence disappeared. In fact, I panicked, my performance was abysmal, and I was cut from the team. That experience taught me that confidence is necessary for success. (A member of that team, Captain Bill McMillan, did go on to win the gold in pistol competition at the Olympics.)

Back on the base, my fellow marines were surprised I didn't score higher on the elite team, they knew I had qualified with an exceptionally high score on the rifle range. Still, they asked for tips on how they could do better. As I was explaining my tactics to them, a sergeant passing through the barracks took note. He called me over and told me about a program they had for people who did not qualify. This program was set up to give compensatory marksmanship training to help those marines qualify next time around. Soon, he introduced me to the captain who had set up the program, who then signed me on to help with the training. I was a little apprehensive because I was only a PFC and some of the men I was assigned to train were officers. My assignment was to coach them during their training period which occurred one week before qualification. I was right on the firing line with them giving helpful suggestions while they were firing at targets. Happily, they all seemed to appreciate my one-on-one advice and I was able to make them feel at ease. Everyone I was assigned to work with qualified that year, including one lieutenant who had never qualified before. Back on base, when I would run into that lieutenant, he would always stop to thank me. You never forget sincere appreciation; it boosts your self-esteem and your confidence. I think it also made me aware of my ability to train others for success.

In the 1970's, I was the Computer Programmer for the Point of Sale (POS) team at Sears, in Philadelphia. POS Point of Sale was leading edge technology at the time. Our objective was to convert each retail store one at a time, from old mechanical cash registers to new computerized POS registers. This new technology involved systemizing all aspects of retail. Sears sent in experts in credit processing, inventory management, sales, commissions, also someone to explain how the new POS cash registers worked. My mission was simple, install the software and instruct the staff, on how to operate their newly installed POS minicomputer. I was onsite day and night. During the day we ran tests on the POS cash registers. The computerized registers captured transactions during normal store hours and transferred them to the minicomputer. Every evening the minicomputer processed and transmitted the days data to a mainframe computer at Sear's central data center.

Those familiar with new system set-ups know that they are fraught with issues to be resolved, and this installation was no different. When things went wrong, I would often spend the entire night trouble shooting problems. When they were resolved I had a lot of time on my hands. I would wander through the store to see how the employees were adapting to the new system as we were getting ready to "go live". During conversations with store employees, I asked them what they thought of the new system? I could tell the older long-time employees were nervous, while the younger ones were excited. They all were loaded with questions, and being a programmer, I understood the entire system, I could answer almost every question. I kept my answers simple, and this approach seemed to put everyone at ease.

Word got to the store manager that I was the go-to-guy for practical answers. He asked me to address a larger group of employees in a more formal way. This request was beyond my assignment, and I could have been in hot water for exceeding my responsibility, but I jumped at the chance. The next day I addressed the group of store personnel and I think it helped relieve some jitters. A week later we activated the new POS system, and all went well. The store manager called my boss and told him he was impressed with my expertise and helpfulness. I believe it was one of the reasons I received my next promotion and transfer back to Sears, Boston, my hometown, and place where my programming career began.

As a new Sears Project Manager, I supervised setting up the retail POS computerization for the New England area. This was a new operation, so we needed to hire people to go out to the stores and do what we did in Philadelphia. We hired young computer technicians, just out of college. They had no experience in this new field of Point of Sale. These young people had to be trained, and once again I was doing exactly what I love to do, training people for success.

Years later, I joined the recruiting firm, Old Colony Group, and I became a Personnel Recruiter, otherwise known as a Headhunter. My boss was a very demanding man, and we didn't see eye to eye. He criticized me for having 'rose colored glasses' because of my positive suggestions to other recruiters. He said that I was too Pollyannaish and soft. He believed you had to be pushy if you were going to succeed. We never got along, and I was very unhappy working for this boss.

However, I quickly became the top Headhunter, and grudgingly I was promoted to Manager. I still had my responsibilities as recruiter, but now the other recruiters reported to me. The first thing I was instructed to do was set up a daily training program for my team. I was happy with this assignment as I was full of ideas that I knew would bring success. Although we never did get along, my boss had the good sense to notice that I had a knack for training people. As a team, we went beyond the company's revenue projections, and year after year we set new records. Training for success made the difference.

In 2000 I was hired as the Telecommunications Coordinator at Children's Hospital, Boston. One year later the hospital started a new program which involved bringing in new IT (Information Technology) interns for training from "Year-Up." The Year-Up program was designed to train disadvantaged young people and help them find significant work in a field where they could have a well-paying job, and an upward career path. At Year-Up they would go through a learning program where they received basic IT training. Children's Hospital, and many other Boston companies would act as good corporate citizens and hire several interns in the IT department for a six-month period. This gave the interns real-world IT experience. If job openings were available at the completion of the internship exemplary interns would be considered for permanent employment.

I was busily involved implementing technology changes and I certainly didn't need any new assignments. However, my boss selected me as the person to train and supervise the interns. Every six months I had new interns to train and manage. Over time, I trained somewhere between 30 and 40 of these young people. I loved every minute of it knowing that I was helping to establish their careers. Now many of them have sought-after positions at Children's Hospital, and others are successfully employed elsewhere. It happened numerous times, and it was always my biggest reward. Former interns would contact me and tell me that my guidance had helped them become successful. I'm also proud that in 2008, Year Up presented me with the Outstanding Supervisor Award for that year.

Chapter 1
Repetition

Repetition is the mother of learning, skill, and habit. This is powerful information because it has shaped and will continue to shape your life. Unrelenting Little Efforts can help you take control and design your life to be as fulfilling as you would like it to be. Whatever thoughts and actions you constantly engage in, they are recorded in your brain, and if they bring pleasure or are necessary, they will become habits. Most of your daily routines are now automatic because you've repeated them so often, they're second nature. Skills such as brushing teeth, driving, typing and a multitude of other activities will not require a second thought.

If what I've just said is true, it means that all along you've been actively practicing the key to success, which is repetition. People who have a strong physique likely know what is meant by the term reps, because that's the major force behind developing muscle. Can you play the piano? If so, you know that even the simplest song requires repetitive practice before it plays out harmoniously. Without repetition you could never learn to swim, ride a bike, or play tennis. I'm sure you can't recall the difficulty you had in learning to read, but unless you are a genius it took years and years for you to become proficient. Even as a baby you had to repeat certain activities over and over before you could walk and talk. I'm sure you believe all this, because if you were going to be operated on you would not want to be the doctors first patient.

All of this should convince you of the old saying "practice makes perfect."

I am active in the stock market now, and I constantly make money, and I'm convinced that anyone can do it, but the price is steep. I've been studying the market for over 25 years, and it took a lot of stumbling and making costly mistakes before I got the hang of it. I have a lot to learn because I still get burned as stocks are incredibly difficult to predict. In fact, the stock market is the most difficult challenge I've ever attempted, and I've tried my hand at many things. Just to survive as a stock trader you must become competent in 4 different areas. Logic, Fundamental - (Financial), Technical - (Charts, and Indicators) and most important Timing. I never applied Psychological Analysis, but I'm sure that would help because it's the reactions of people that moves the market. I'm not making a fortune, but the so-called Wall Street Wizards make millions every year. If I want to join that elite group, I know I must dig in and study those four areas with more intense repetition than I'm currently willing to do. The key word in that last sentence is repetition. You need to repeat and know the subject as well as you know your own name. Don't be deceived, doing all that would be worthless without the buying and selling of stocks, the repetitive correction of mistakes is what's needed to learn.

The point of all this is not to get you involved in stock trading. Success in any endeavor is your choice, but you must first make a firm commitment, and absolutely set aside the necessary time for whatever you would like to do. You can learn, and with enough repetition even master abilities such as guitar, tennis, writing, dance, technology, memory, bodybuilding, mathematics, oil painting, you name it. Warren Buffet said it best: "Intensity is the price of excellence"

Chapter 2
Belief

"Belief is one of the most powerful organic forces in the multiverse. It may not be able to move mountains, exactly. But it can create someone who can."

Terry Pratchett

I hope to fire up your belief for the most exciting future you can imagine, and then spur you on to action so that you can live it. A big part of achieving success is the strong belief that it is possible for you to do the thing you want to do. You're reading this so I am certain you can execute other complicated skills, for example driving, typing, swimming, cooking, etc. Anything that required some effort on your part to learn, proves you have a track record for success. Whatever abilities you've acquired all started with the belief that you could succeed. It's a simple formula, you believed, attempted, persisted, and you now have the skill desired. This is the successful foundation you can build upon. Now think back, and you may remember that once you were convinced that you could do the thing, there was no stopping you! My point is that you are an amazing, talented, go-getter once you know you can do something. When belief takes possession of your mind you are empowered to do things that once seemed impossible. The energy from this feeling of certainty makes you a force to be reckoned with. When you've convinced yourself, you then have the ability to make things happen. That's the power of belief.

Look around and see the marvels of man's creations, huge planes above defying gravity, cell phones sending wireless messages all over the world, entertainment and sports watched from home on huge screens, and everyone's aware that we've landed on the moon. I'm sure that you could describe many more things like this that once were considered impossible. Think about this, someone first had to believe that man could fly, send pictures through the air, and walk on the moon, before any of these things could happen. The power of belief can be verified by the billions of impossible things that at one time did not exist, but now are everywhere you look.

Believers are still at it; visualize a flying car, that does not need a runway, it takes off straight up, and lands straight down, has no jets or external propellers, and runs on electricity. I'll tell you more, but first imagine this: Your about to be operated on and the surgeon shows you a tiny robot that will be inserted in your body by way of a slight incision in your belly. This surgeon then shows you an audio-visual headset that will be on this doctor's head during your surgery. Before you go under anesthesia you see that the doctor's hands have all sorts of finger sensors that will control the robot. In one sense the doctor will become the robot, looking through the robot's eyes seeing inside your body, controlling the tiny robot, and fixing your problem. You don't believe it? I want you to be a believer so you can now see both amazing innovations on YouTube. The flying car was created by Lilium, the little robot by Vicarious Surgical, and you can find both videos under those names. If you're a stock investor check out the tickers LILM and RBOT.

What does all of this mean for your life? With self-belief, you can have the career you want, you can pursue the life you desire. The only one you must convince is you, then it's all within your reach. Belief starts in your mind; you see yourself doing the thing. Now act and with persistence what you've imagined becomes your reality.

Chapter 3
Choice

"What you do today can improve all your tomorrows."

Ralph Marston

Today Your Life Begins Anew! We are all the total of our choices; there can be no doubt about that, we've designed the life we are now living. In the beginning we had no choices, we could not determine our birthplace, parents, or genetic makeup, but since those early days, barring accidents, we've been in charge. If you're perfectly happy, keep doing what you're doing, you've made good choices. Then again, maybe you're asking yourself; what was I thinking, I could have made so many better choices. It's true that superior choices could have improved your health, wealth, and happiness, and starting today you can decide to make high quality choices. You have it within your power to reverse many bad decisions. If a decision or situation can't be reversed, you can still find a joyous way to live. If you're not satisfied with your current situation that can be a blessing. Strong dissatisfaction can be the jolt you need to compel you to start making the good choices that will brighten your days ahead. Never underestimate yourself, you are an awesome force in this world because you have the power to choose. Not an hour goes by that you don't employ this force to make some little change in your life. Even the most minor choices are adding up by days, weeks, months, and years. If your good choices outweigh bad choices, you're probably happy with the life you're living. And if you're not pleased, this moment can be your opportunity. Little by little you can start moving towards a life that brings constant fulfillment, because it is always getting better.

Let's discuss the strategy and tactics needed so that you can live your best possible life. At this current moment, look at your accomplishments, the places you've gone, and the possessions you have. Observing these facts, gives you a giant clue as to how you've arrived at where you are. We come right back to choices, don't we? It's obvious choosing is the power that created your current circumstances. This knowledge should convince you that the same process can determine your future. Looked at from this point of view it's almost like magic. Step one you need a clear idea of what you want. Step two make a firm decision to go after it with intensity.

What if you have no idea of what you want, not a clue as to the dream life that would make you happy? There is an answer to this dilemma and hopefully it will interest and inspire you. You simply need to become a dreamer. Sit back, relax, and dream about a lifestyle that would appeal to you. You'll feel on top of the world once you find something to be excited about. All accomplishment starts with something that is best described as a dream. It doesn't yet exist, but just the fact that you can imagine it means you can bring it into existence. Because it's your dream, it will fire up your desire and generate enthusiasm. You'll have a dreamer's passion and you'll be willing to do the things you need to do. Now if you can make a real commitment to get started, you will have determined your destiny.

This thought must have crossed your mind. What's the downside? It will take time to do this. Yes, but it's an upbeat time as you anticipate the nicer life you're moving towards. You always have more energy when you're moving in the direction of your dreams. Take solace in the fact that many of the world's high achievers have said their journey was more enjoyable than the final achievement.

Don't be afraid to think big, in this book you will find scientific reasons to believe that all the power you need resides within you. A chemist in a lab can combine two mildly effective chemicals and get a much more powerful reaction than either of the chemicals could produce alone. That's similar to combining two potent human powers, a dream and an action. United they become a superpower and produce life changing results. If this formula is repeated over and over it will bring a dream into reality. Your vision of an exciting career, a nice home, a dream car, an amazing vacation, can become reality once you're committed to action, and unrelenting follow through. Without the vital element of continuous action, dreams that could have been realized go up in smoke.

How can you possibly start without knowing in advance everything that's involved and account for all the things that need to be done? That question represents the intimidating wall that stops the smart, strong, and willful from reaching their dreams. It's deceptive because it's really not a barrier, it's just an illusion. The answer to this impasse is simple. You take the most obvious first step and the next step becomes clear, and on and on. You can speed up the process and eliminate many steps by making a plan. Your plan can be as simple or detailed as needed to meet your needs and natural tendencies.

Courage is what you need to start your one step at a time journey. Right before your eyes all you've imagined will begin to appear. Amazing, unexpected things will happen once you're in action. You attract people who assist you, everyone and everything moves in your favor.

"Whatever you can do, or dream you can, begin it. Boldness has genius, power and magic in it."
Goethe.

Your intense desire finds a way to overcome obstacles. Once you've decided where you want to go, perseverance keeps you on course. At some point you will be happily living the dream life you imagined.

Now, let's not forget how we got here. Take a deep breath and think about what led you to this enjoyable way of life. Your current reality and your future are controlled by your thoughts and actions. When you reflect on this process that has shaped your life, you know it will continue to do so. It's all very clear now that if you make the best choices it will lead to rewarding outcomes. Good decisions can multiply like rabbits and bring wonderful visions into reality. Know for sure, the simple act of choosing wisely can shape life to your satisfaction. Our choices today will determine how well we live tomorrow.

This is not complicated, there is a simple way for you to take control and make good choices. The following sentence really works: "Is this a good choice or a bad choice?" It is a simple sentence but don't be deceived, it's like putting Aladdin's Lamp in your hands. Asking this question causes you to seek your own advice before making a snap decision. What happens when you ask this question? Each time you make a choice you will most often make the best choice. In time you will have a mountain of good decisions, and from the top of that mountain the day's ahead will look much brighter. This is worth repeating, wonderful tomorrows are built on the choices we make today.

Obviously, making wise choices is a good idea, but many good ideas you will find are in a worthless junk-pile, never having been applied. Then again, good ideas put into action can amass a fortune. The automatic practice of making good decisions must become our daily habit. Remember repetition is the mother of learning, skill, and habit.

How can we lock this simple sentence into memory? "Is this a good choice or a bad choice?" Sometimes it takes a world-shaking event to plant a memory firmly into our brain cells. The pandemic horribly affected all of us, but we can derive something good out of it. Yes, we're going to use this event to help us to remember to ask: "Is this a good choice or a bad choice?" Every time you Wash Your Hands it will be the trigger you need to start making your best choices. As you wash the germs and viruses from your hands you simply ask yourself this question: "Is this a good choice or a bad choice?" Doing this often, will implant the question in your mind, and it can be a positive life changing event, that makes you aware of your daily choices.

An abundance of good choices will help you grow mentally, physically, and financially. It's just a simple reminder, you've always had the power to choose, and now with this question embedded in your brain, you're more alert to making the very best choices. Soon there will be no doubt, as your good choices pile up taking you to the wonderful future you've always wanted.

Now you're convinced, you see it growing real by the moment. And to think all you had to do was to choose.

Chapter 4
Emotional Power

"Moons and Junes and Ferris wheels
The dizzy dancing way you feel
As every fairy tale comes real"

From a song by Joni Mitchell

Let's go to that time in your life when your mind swirled with excitement. Your common everyday surroundings sparkled as though you were in a magical wonderland. You were enjoying life to the full because you fell in love. Totally focused on the person who made you feel this way, life was perfect.

Only one thing could focus the mind to this level of obsession, the biological force we call the sex drive. Now we're going to discover how this force can keep our life expanding in wonderful ways. Like breathing, eating, and sleeping, sex is a pleasurable act. I'm sure you don't think about this very often, but everyone you know, and love is the result of the sex act. Thank your lucky stars, you would not be reading this except that two people decide to have sex. This powerful drive causes us to feel ecstasy and has brought us all into existence.

There is an actual physical location for this driving force. It's in our brain, and it's not very big considering the important role nature assigned it to play. It's the size and shape of an almond, two almonds in fact, one for each hemisphere of the brain. Known as the Amygdala, this miniscule area of the brain is always on alert for anything that will help us survive. It triggers anger, fear, and sexual desire. The Amygdala is evolutionary, it traces back to what is known as the reptilian or limbic brain. Nature has always provided living creatures with survival emotions, even a spider will run for its life if it senses danger. One of the primary tasks nature assigned the Amygdala was to make sure we would go forth and multiply. And what an amazing record of accomplishment, there are over 7 billion of us now on the planet. Still like the energizer bunny the Amygdala keeps on going, sending us little pulses to always be on the alert for danger and opportunities.

Can we harness this force for Super Motivation? I think we can. Everyone would like a more interesting, enjoyable, and successful life. But it's so hard for most people to get moving; beyond having to perform the daily necessities of life. They think to themselves why am I so lazy, I know I should be doing this that or the other. That lethargy can lift in an instant if there is a reward within reach. Let me ask you: When you know that something wonderful is about to happen in your life, are you energized? I'm fairly certain your answer is yes.

I think you'll agree that there's not much chance a person purchasing a lottery ticket will win the big prize. Yet, a lot of people are excited imagining what they're going to do when they win. I'm sure you've noticed that the bigger the lottery pot grows, the longer the lines to buy tickets. Yet, the chance of winning is close to zero. It's amazing how imagining a reward can stimulate a person to act, especially when the reward is big. Instinctively we know that action is the foundation of all success. That's why people buying lottery tickets will repeat the old cliché: You've got to be in it to win it."

Let's see what you and I together can learn from this observation. Anticipation of a reward is what gets us to spring into action. This is particularly true when the reward is spectacular. Do you have an idea or a desire to do something that will bring you success? That's wonderful, because now we're going to supercharge your motivation to get moving and doing. It's not going to be all that hard to do. Take the time to convince yourself that a big exciting reward is just around the corner, and you'll be as supercharged as the people in line for lottery tickets, but your chances of winning big will be far greater than zero.

Think Big, google those words and you'll find them mentioned numerous times by successful people. It's likely you know of Richard Branson, here's what he has to say: "If people aren't calling you crazy you aren't thinking big enough." Keep bouncing the reward ball back and forth in your mind, and you'll find yourself in a state of super motivation.

Now you know how to generate all the energy you'll ever need; you just anticipate a big, to any one and now you're in the club. All you have to do is act the way successful people act. Successful people burst through the walls of fear, fatigue and reluctance, because they're chasing big rewards, certain that they will catch up with them. I know you've done this at some level, because all people are moved to action even when the reward they seek is relatively small. The smallest reward imagined will generate an amount of energy equal to the task. The trick to releasing this energy is to believe that it is possible.

Women go to the hairdresser because they are convinced that people will notice and admire them. Men don't go to a gym just because they feel the need to do hard work. They go because they imagine in advance that it will improve their physical appearance, and of course their health. Kids convince their parents to buy expensive sneakers because they imagine how cool they'll look to their friends. These imagined rewards are moving the whole world all the time. When a woman spends a lot of time picking out a dress, it's not so much the quality of the material that's important to her, it's the idea that others will find her attractive. I think you'll agree, all these people are in action because they have a reward in mind. They're energized by their own expectations.

Now the exciting life that you've always wanted is within your grasp. We are all equipped with natures powerful energy switch, the Amygdala. All you have to do is take a minute to flip your energy switch on. It's easy, just decide to go after a reward that excites you. Wow! Thinking about the reward that you desire has you energized with emotional power. Act, and you are on your way to a fabulous new life.

Chapter 5
Your Ultimate Advantage

"The human brain has 100 billion neurons, each neuron connected to 10 thousand other neurons. Sitting on your shoulders is the most complicated object in the known universe."

Michio Kaku

You my friend are in possession of one of these marvels. You're more advanced and have more built-in genetic intelligence than any other species on this planet. Human brain power has put you at the top of life's food chain. So, let's discuss your intellect. It's most likely that I've never met you, but still I'm convinced that you have a working cerebral cortex. How do I know that? Because you can instantly decipher this extremely complicated code you're looking at. I know also that you are a mind reader because you are now reading what's on my mind. You are a little slow because these were the thoughts in my mind a while back. In fact, I know that you are super intelligent because you had the good sense to pick up this book which will change your life for the better. We humans don't have the slightest idea of what the bounds of human potential are because we are continually testing the limits. However, I'm sure that after you engage and explore the ideas in this book; your own intellect will illuminate more of your own personal potential and possibilities. It is to your advantage in life to be fully aware of the awesome power that you have in your brain. Being a former Marine, one of the first things we had to learn in the Marine Corps was the nomenclature of each rifle part. We had to learn how to assemble and disassemble this weapon. This was important because a working knowledge of our rifle would increase our chance of survival. That was vital information we had to learn. If we were as regimented as Marines, we surely would be obligated to learn about the brain because it's the survival mechanism for everyday life. It's interesting that very few of us understand this organ that controls our life. Let's stand back and look at the architecture of this wonder. It's a round blob of gray matter that is directing your whole life. Your brain is likely about the size of most other brains, weighing somewhere between 2.7 to 3.3 lbs. It's always running, and the fuel it runs on is blood glucose. It's a relatively small body part; it comprises about 2% of your body's mass. This little thinking organ has a good appetite because it consumes around 25% of the body's total fuel. Thinking is hard work, and that fuel consumption amounts to around 20% of your caloric intake. You're probably taking a deep breath because of all these technicalities; that's good because your brain needs about one fifth of the oxygen you breath to keep on thinking. In fact, these details are trivial points of interest, the important thing for you to understand is that you have the brainpower to make your life everything you've ever wanted. I want you to realize that your ultimate advantage in life is your brain. The human brain has the power to communicate, invent, and solve problems. You have a brilliant brain, and this book is intended to implant success ideas in that brain that will bloom into your success story. Together we'll team up and put your prodigious brainpower to work. This will guarantee that you will live a great life worthy of a genius with a brain like yours.

Chapter 6
DNA, Built-In Intelligence

"Action is the real measure of intelligence."

Napoleon Hill

Can you be sure you have the unlimited potential to reach your dreams? It's a reasonable question, no one wants to make a good effort to no avail. I'll give you the answer right now, it's an unmitigated yes. How can I be so sure? I'll approach my answer from a purely logical standpoint. As a former computer programmer, I have a tremendous respect for logic, because a computer will only produce good results from perfect logic.

Mushrooms, crickets, camels, birds, roses, and all of us have something in common, DNA. What exactly is DNA? It's nature's programming language responsible for producing all the different forms of life on earth. Much of this life has intelligence, and humans have come out on top as the most intelligent. Birds have intelligence, they know how to build their nest. Bees have this same genetic aptitude; you've seen the hives in which they live. If that doesn't impress you, how long would it take you to build a nest or hive? Even little ants have knowledge that enables them to act as tiny engineers.

The lowly housefly has intelligence based on this remarkable DNA programming. Just how intelligent is the fly? Well the fly can fly of course, but it can also see, crawl, find food and even copulate with other flies. You say you're not too impressed with the fly's intelligence. The next time you use your hand to swat one, see who comes out ahead. Are you still convinced the fly is dumb? Well, we smart humans have not been able to create a computer chip with the intelligence of a housefly. Man will at some point be able to put that much intelligence on a chip because we're the only life form that keeps adding to our current knowledge.

Of all the creatures on this planet only humans actively seek to grow smarter, yet it is almost certain that we are living below our full capability. Thomas A. Edison who many would think of as a person who lived up to his full potential had this to say: "If we all did the things we are really capable of doing, we would literally astound ourselves." I wanted to bring this to your attention hoping I can encourage you to challenge yourself to attain what you desire. It's in your DNA, you have the built-in intelligence to succeed.

Chapter 7
Imagination

"Our greatest weakness lies in giving up. The most certain way to succeed is always to try just one more time."

Thomas A. Edison

Join Me on this Imaginary Adventure. Listen to people when they talk about how they feel so pressured with all the everyday demands of life. They'd like to escape at least for a while. They all want something better than what they now have. What's stopping them. If we could find the answer to that we'd be able to help them get what they want. We know the answers don't come easy.

The answers we're looking for possibly exist somewhere in the fantastic world of imagination. Imagination only exists in the mind where everything is possible and there are no limits. Has anyone ever tried to go directly into the mind knowing they would not be bound by the restrictions in the real world?

Let's do it, come with me on this adventure and we'll be the first to travel into the mind and visit the unexplored realm of imagination. Here we go, we're now walking inside the mind of a typical person. Wow, being in the mind is strange, it feels like forbidden territory doesn't it? Incredible, just you and me on this adventure. I'll bet we have the same feelings as the astronauts when they first landed on the moon.

Since we're the first ones to explore like this we have to be careful but imagine what we can discover. Look over there, at that wall! I've never seen anything like it, have you? A structure so huge, look at the words written on it, so chilling. "Wall of Impossibility Stay Out! Your Life is At Risk!" I'm assuming that everyone has a wall like this in their mind to protect them from unseen danger.

I know we shouldn't tempt fate, but I want to know more. You don't have to come with me unless you want to. I'm going over to see it close up. Oh my god, my hand goes right through the wall. It's just an illusion. It doesn't really exist. This is just too weird maybe we should get out of here. Are you telling me you'd like to explore more because we might learn something valuable? I think you're right since we're here we should try to find important answers to life's secrets. We may never get another chance like this. I see a road over there that looks interesting. Look up at the street sign-Decision Road. This is odd, the road is paved like the legendary Yellow Brick Road, except it's paved with diamond shaped field stone. Interesting, the diamond shape is the symbol for decision on a programmer's flow chart. As we travel down this road you can feel a certain atmospheric pressure. So unusual it's like we're on another planet. Let's keep going because if we can find just one answer that will help people, we'll be real heroes, we might even go down in history.

Going through a person's mind is weird and wonderful, it's such an adventure. Have you noticed the odd names on the side roads leading off Decision Road? There's one sign over there that reads "Later" and we just passed two others "Not Now" and "Soon." Look up ahead there's another sign "Tomorrow." Hey look, Decision Road comes to an end at this fork. Great, I was getting the feeling we would never get off this road, I look forward to the change of scenery.

Ocean Road goes down to the right, and Now Road goes up and to the left. Ocean Road brings a picture of pleasure to my mind, it's so alluring. Now Road looks difficult, it's an uphill climb. This is an easy decision, let's go down Ocean Road.

I can see the ocean, it's not what I expected. Look down from the edge of this cliff. It looks turbulent like a boiling ocean. It's frightening. Can you see those shark fins? Now look close to shore, if you look carefully, you can detect those little fish swimming near the shore. Those are barracuda; they'll eat you alive faster than any shark could. Look out near the horizon, I can see dark thunder clouds and bolts of lightning striking down. It's like no ocean I've ever seen, and I don't smell the wonderful sea air I sense at beaches I know. I wouldn't swim or sail in these waters for any amount of money.

Well we've decided to do this so let's be brave and venture closer just for the sake of discovery. Look over here at the edge of this cliff, can you see the sign? Be careful there's loose gravel under our feet, we could slip down. The sign says, "Ocean of Dread, No Swimming" I want to get closer to the sign, there's some small writing below the warning I want to see. "This is an ocean of undone tasks, and you're about to fall in." Oops! I can feel my feet slipping out from under me, let's get out of here. Big mistake: we should have chosen Now Road. This is getting much too dangerous, and I don't know if we're learning anything. Let's backtrack the way we came in, we'll go back down Decision Road to the

"Wall of Impossible," it's right at the point where we entered.

It's time we escaped from this mysterious world. Now that we're on the way back we can relax a little. Guess what, it just hit me, we did learn something after all. It's not that obvious, but I had an epiphany. Travelling through the mind, we accidently stumbled across a hidden truth, that will help everyone to have less stress. Think for a moment isn't this exactly what we learned? "Decide Now or Drown!"

Look I can see the "Wall of Impossible," It looks to be less than a mile from here, and we're moving quickly. Ah, at last we've arrived. Nothing around the wall looks familiar. Do you remember exactly where we came in? Neither do I. Don't tell me! Could it be that we can't return? I hope we didn't violate some rule of the universe about staying out of the sanctuary of the mind. We don't want to be trapped in here forever. Maybe this wall is really telling us that it's impossible for us to get out. Perhaps what we've learned is that some things truly are impossible, like escaping from here. Should we sit down, accept our fate, and die. Let's at least try one more thing.

We know the wall itself is an illusion; I put my hand through it. Let's walk through the "Wall of Impossible," hopefully we won't perish in doing so. We'll see where it leads.

Wonderful! Fabulous! Marvelous! Look! right, left, up, down, everywhere, all you can see are possibilities. More possibilities than stars in the sky. Like you, I thought we were doomed, but we didn't let the wall stop us, I can see the way, we're going home. Can you believe it, we've survived, and we've learned some valuable lessons. This is a big win, our journey through the mind has proved to be a valuable expedition.

We've arrived home with three great discoveries. First we learned, impossible is just an illusion, then we found a way to improve life every day. "Decide Now or Drown." That statement points out that we will drown in a stream of never-ending little tasks if we don't handle them-Now! Finally, we discovered this great truth, never give up because: "We are never trapped, we can always find a way to win."

Chapter 8
Thoughts

"Our life always expresses the result of our dominant thoughts."

Soren Kierkegaard

As long as we are alive these three things will be constant: heartbeat, breathing, and thinking. Only thinking makes our life meaningful. It controls our actions and determines how we interact with others. Ultimately the power of our thinking establishes how much we enjoy this one-time miracle, life. In one sense our thoughts are the essence of life itself, truly we live in our mind.

We're alive with thoughts that stir our emotions and create our reality. If all your thoughts disappeared would you still exist? Our thoughts make us conscious of everything that affects us. This awareness activates our emotions, warns us of danger and alerts us to opportunities. The passion of our thoughts determines the strength of our emotions. Strong emotions are the driving force that compel us to act.

Properly directed our dominant thoughts can protect us, and insure we have a happy high-quality life. When life is threatened in any way our emotional power is at its peak, survival is the highest priority. This is especially true when masses of people unite with one dominate thought, to confront a common danger. This unified emotive power is on display now as this book is being written.

The Covid 19 pandemic is upon us, devastating, disruptive, and causing a great loss of life. When life and death are at stake our response is always swift, and most often successful.

We will prevail over this plague because we have faced crisis after crisis and still we survive. Our resolve has been tested so our confidence is justified.

In the 1940's during World War II the United States and our allies faced the possibility of mass annihilation. The United States was at war with Germany and Japan, these three countries were in a race to create the world's first atomic bomb. It was assumed that the first country to develop this doomsday weapon would likely win World War II.

The US government was so concerned about our enemies acquiring and using this weapon against us that a massive program called the Manhattan Project was launched to develop the ultimate bomb. Inventing and assembling a nuclear warhead would prove to be extremely complex, its possibility only existed in the minds of physicists. Our survival would be decided within the crucible of this undertaking. With no guarantees of success thousands of scientists, engineers, physicists, and other prodigies were assembled to see if such a weapon could be developed.

The historic result, in 1945 two weapons of mass destruction were dropped over Japan killing thousands and ending World War II. This momentous occurrence put the world on notice of the possibility of human extinction by our own hand. Wars between nations continue, but it is encouraging to note that never again have nuclear weapons been used in warfare. Survival is still the human priority and currently the world believes in mutually assured destruction. Life is so precious that we all want to keep on living.

Now our current threat is the deadly virus, it needs to be met with the same resolve. Fortunately for us we have a team of dedicated medical experts determined to conquer this menace to life. Our brilliant medical scientists are single-mindedly focused on finding a cure and they will do it in record time. We all instinctively know that this herculean effort to find a cure will succeed.

The Covid19 pandemic shifted the focus of this chapter from individual thinking, to masses of people synchronized in their thoughts because they face a common danger. The theme of this chapter has not changed. The central idea is that thoughts are powerful, and evidence all around us proves that thoughts can change the world and create new realities. Let us return to the original purpose of this chapter, which was to improve the individual's world, through the power of thinking.

The mind contains our thoughts, and it is so powerful you may not believe some of the things I'm about to tell you. Your mind is a time machine; although an imperfect one. I'm sure you've gone back into the past, thinking of those memorable times in your life that inspired and made you happy. Have you also gone back remembering arguments, and other disturbing mistakes that made you feel miserable? We would all like to change the past, but our time machine has a slight flaw. When we travel back in time we cannot change anything that has happened. So let's not do that anymore, only go back when we want to reminisce the good times. Hopefully, important lessons learned will not be forgotten. Luckily with our time machine we can also time-travel into the future. Again, because our time machines are not perfect, we will not be able to speed up our arrival. Happily, we can plan desirable changes we'll make when we get there. I told you this would be a little hard to believe, but there is still more to this mind power that you possess. I don't know where on earth you are located, but at this very minute I am transmitting my thoughts to you, and you being a mind-reader are receiving them exactly as I transmit them. Yes, of course you are reading, but we are connected mentally as if we were sitting in the same room. It's just one more amazing example of how the power of your thoughts can make your world a little better, maybe a lot better.

I have entitled this chapter 'Thoughts,' intending to elevate the importance of thoughts to their rightful place in our life. We must always be aware that our thoughts are the lifeblood of our existence. Try to argue against this precept and you will find that it is impossible, but it will also convince you, if you need convincing. Thoughts activate our emotions and emotions spur us on to do the things we do. Our thoughts have created the life we're now living.

In this material world, only when our thoughts convert into actions do we truly change our way of life. The ultimate use of mind power is to imagine the desirable future you want for yourself and your loved ones. You need to start by expecting the best, otherwise you will never get started. Nature did not design us to venture into doubtful arenas that will not work in our best interest.

Your expectations have a lot to do with how much success in life you will enjoy. Low expectations leave you tired with no energy or desire to do anything. On the other hand, high expectations have you looking forward to something that will make you happy. When you're absolutely convinced things will turn out the way you want, this pumps up your energy. You're excited, and you have a willingness to do whatever is necessary to make it happen. This is the attitude of successful people and when you have it, you just can't help feeling good.

What if you expect the best and it doesn't work out? It's likely you have just come upon a temporary detour. Obstacles are not new to you, all your life you've experienced them. I can say this to all readers; you're not unique everyone hits obstacles. No matter how skilled and knowledgeable you become you will always be facing temporary blockades at times, it's to be expected; in other words that's life.

Success comes from being able to go around obstacles to find a better way of going to where you want to go and getting what you want to get. If you lay down when you should be striving to go forward you will never get anywhere. Remember you will endure the same amount of suffering whether you fail or succeed, so you might as well struggle to succeed. All you need is a new set of thoughts to face the challenge, now you're on your way to a brighter day.

We used the analogy of the time machine to make the point that we can go back and view the past and we know we can also imagine our future. This brings us to the realization that we spend a large part of our life not actually experiencing the moment, but instead imagining what was or what will be. Many times, when we live the experience we've imagined we find we were happier in the dream than we are in the actual event.

Since we're going to be living a good portion of life in our imagination, we should make sure it's going to be a good place to live. Feeling good is the result of living successfully, when life is a pleasure it's because we're managing to live in a way that makes us happy. This brings us right back to the importance of our thoughts and our thinking. If we spend a lot of our time thinking depressing thoughts, we know how that's going to make us feel. Remember anticipating a nice vacation, or driving the car you've always wanted, or hoping for a wonderful new love relationship. You know the euphoria you feel from that kind of expectation. It's hard to believe but it's all in your imagination. No matter, it makes you incredibly happy, and the best part is that with this type of illusion you are setting the stage for it to really happen.

Thinking can pave the way for the wonderful life you would like to lead, and it can keep you joyfully involved in your fantasy, but only your actions can bring that world into reality. If you have a commitment to action, the odds of your success are immense.

Now to complete the picture of you enjoying a successful life you need a written plan. To expect results without a plan of action would be like trying to go on a distant vacation without money, car, or GPS. In life, you must know where you're going and how you're going to get there. Without a doubt, following a plan of action will lead you to living the good life. Realistically, it will not be smooth sailing all the way. You must be prepared to deal with anything that impedes your progress.

This means your plan will have to be modified often for you to arrive at your destination. A plan needs to be simple, in fact the simpler the plan the better, because it needs to be changed over and over again as you go along. By adjusting your plan, you stay on course. In time, the plan will become crystal clear and more believable.

On the rarest of occasions, the objective you're seeking may turn out to be unrealistic. All is not lost, you have gained valuable information from lessons learned, and you can use that knowledge to speed your progress towards something more attainable. When you know what you want and you're going after it, you're all excited in anticipation. In this highly charged emotional state you're willing to pay the price required to live your dream.

Getting what you want is hard work, but if you know the formula for winning in life, you're encouraged to keep on going. It's a pretty simple formula: One-Plan, Two-Act, Three-Adjust the plan. One, Two, Three, over and over, at some point you will arrive.

What is the most important thing you need to do to bring about the wonderful life you dream of? It's getting started, there's no question about that. Once you're in action you're automatically enrolled in the world of do-ers, and you can expect to be rewarded. We get what we want when we stick to something. The only way you can lose is to quit before you arrive. Probably the most important lesson we learn in life is don't quit. Vince

Lombardy said: "Winners never quit, and quitters never win" and it's true.

Chapter 9
Psyching Up on Sun Power

"If you have a dream, don't just sit there. Gather courage to believe that you can succeed and leave no stone unturned to make it a reality"

Dr. Roopleen

Where can you ever find the abundant energy you need to live the wonderful life you desire? Well did you ever think about this; you are running on the sun's energy. Every time you eat, you are fueling up on energy that came from the sun. Plants absorb the suns energy, and all life's creatures eat the plants to get energy. The next time you see a BLT on your plate know that you're about to get a nice supply of energy from the sun. Also consider yourself lucky because you're at the top of the food chain, otherwise you might be at the wrong side of the dinner table, providing the sun's energy instead of gaining it.

Not only do we get our energy from the sun, but just about everything you see moving on planet earth is running on sun power. Our cars, trucks, and busses would all be stuck in the mud if it wasn't for sun power. The jets that fly off into the sunlight are flying on sunlight. We don't think much about it because it all started long before you and I were around. It happened even before the dinosaurs appeared on earth. The energy you get from plugging in the toaster, or microwave, came down from the sun 300 million years ago. It was captured by the prehistoric plants that were growing in those early days. Over eons of time those plants we call fossils got converted into coal, oil, and gas. Excluding nuclear, all the energy that makes your life so easy and wonderful came from that big bright ball of light up there in the sky. What does it all mean to you?

Whether you want to walk, run, drive, or fly, no matter how you want to get there, your dream life is waiting. The sun did its part, it has given you all the energy you're ever going to need. You've got sun power, now it's up to you. It raises a big question, doesn't it? Why do so many people who are full of the sun's life-giving energy, feel so tired, weary, and unenergetic?

In this chapter you'll get the answer to that big question. You've kept reading so I know we're on the same wavelength, we both know that perseverance leads to success. We're so much alike, we just met, and it's like we're old friends. This life-giving sun power we all run on is mighty energy, it's the same sun energy that fuels almost all of the powerhouse turbines that produce electricity. Mostly it's potential energy, meaning you must release it. No sense leaving this valuable gift from Old Sol dormant, it's time to put it to work for you. It can be fun thinking about all the great things you'll enjoy doing when once you tap into this life force. Enjoy imagining the things you can have once you get moving. Armed with the knowledge, your about to receive, you can use this power to be all you've wanted to be. Imagine the great person you're about to become. Now enjoy, take some time to decide where you want to go, what you want to do, who you want to be. Of course, you could decide to lay on the couch and do nothing, but I know you'd feel miserable thinking about all the good times you missed.

Now to answer the big question, how can we overcome any lack of energy, and get access to the abundant energy we know that exists. What do we often do when we want to leave boredom and dissatisfaction behind? We entertain ourselves by watching a movie or take in a sporting event. Why do we do this? It's because we want to see somebody releasing their energy doing some of the great things, we know we'd enjoy doing. Check this out, you've released your own vital energy rooting for the hero in a movie.

Let's go there now. Totally involved your heart is pumping, your adrenalin is surging through your veins, excitement is going full blast, who cares if it's only make believe. Sometimes you know better than the person in the movie as to what they should be doing. All your juices are flowing, it's frustrating you've got the power and you know what to do, but you're stuck in your seat. Sometimes it gets so real you jump out of your seat. If only you could jump into the movie you could be the hero, you know what to do and you've got what it takes. It's a downright shame, they should have put you in the movie, and pay you what they're paying this superstar.

Well now you know, you've got what it takes to be a big success. Now I think we're on to something, you've been good at releasing energy at will all your life. You are great at getting all psyched up over other people's success. Watching a good movie you have no lack of energy, no hesitation, you join right in, you're a full-fledged participant in the escapade. No matter how difficult the challenge you stick with it all the way, you're no quitter. You've got the same feelings and drive as if it were real. Don't be embarrassed this is really you, you've got the power, the smarts, the courage, you've got it all. Now all you have to do is get excited about your own adventure, start planning your life's thrilling journey. When an athlete or team you're cheering for wins, you feel the same exhilaration as the players, and you enjoy the victory as much as they do. You've got to admit, it's a little strange, you're doing it from a comfortable chair with little or no sweat.

Let's analyze this to see how you can make sensational things happen in your life, just like in the movies. What's the one vital thing all movie stars and athletes possess before they get into action. The answer is they have a screenplay, we'll call it their game plan. The director or coach is there to make sure everyone follows the script. How strange, and weird would it be if everyone wandered around not knowing what they should be doing. Not much energy is needed by people without a plan, or goal. They just drift around letting life happen to them. With no plan the most capable people are like leaves blowing in the wind. When you know where you want to go, and you have something exhilarating to look forward to you will be instantly energized.

Planning makes you feel good, it's like a coming attraction that gives you a glimpse of how great your life is going to be. People who are successful have big plans. The guiding principle is simple they want to be the best. Most will tell you that their aim was high, some state it quietly, others boastfully e.g. Mohammed Ali: "*I am the greatest!*" A lofty plan will need constant adjustment, but your objective should be rock solid and never change. It's easy to believe in a plan that you create, and belief is vital. When it's your plan, no one can tell you what to do. As this chapter points out, you have energy derived from the sun; only a small trickle is needed to keep you alive. Nature's top priority is survival, so most of your energy is conserved to protect you in this uncertain world. If you were drowning in the ocean and spotted a life-raft within reach, there would be no lack of energy; have no doubt you would reach that raft. Planning puts you in control of your energy. It lets you tap into your vast store of power, enabling you to prosper. Your plan primes the energy pump and follow through action releases the energy. Instantly you are exhilarated with the joy of living while chasing your dream. What happened? You've just become the hero in your own real-life movie. You're on fire with desire there's no stopping you. Tell me, you're not the least bit tired now, are you? That's because you're participating in the sun bright future you wanted. This movie has a happy ending, your dream becomes reality.

Chapter 10
Brain Power

"You have brains in your head. You have feet in your shoes. You can steer yourself in any direction you choose. You're on your own, and you know what you know. And you are the guy who'll decide where to go."

Dr. Seuss

It's hard to believe that this squishy little sphere, the human brain, thought up all the man-made things surrounding you at this moment, but of course it did. We really have no precise way of measuring how much information, or how many memories we can store in our brain, but from what we do know we can make some guesses.

The human brain's neurons, commonly called brain cells, are estimated to number somewhere around 85 to 100 billion cells. By comparison, the brain cells of a baboon number only 14 billion. That's probably why we call them baboons. The brain goes beyond just being a computing device because the brain has achieved consciousness. So comparing the brain to a computer, which has no concept of self, is absurd. Still it's an interesting comparison, so let's do it. Many experts believe that the technological advances and prosperity we enjoy today were predicted in 1965 by Moore's Law. Moore's law states that the number of transistors on a computer chip will double about every 24 months. We are in the year 2020 and the most advanced chip has 1.2 trillion transistors on it. If we look back just a few years to 2015 we see the number of transistors on a chip were at 7.1 billion proving that Moore's law has been validated. Comparing computer chips to brain cells is really a stretch. It's like comparing a car to a horse when we talk about horsepower. Knowing that transistors on a chip do not have the same type of intelligence as brain cells we'll make the best guesses one can make comparing computer power to brain power. We can start by saying that our current computers even with advanced artificial intelligence have nowhere near the smarts of our friend the baboon. It would take 10 terabytes of computer storage to store all of the information in the Library of Congress. It's been guesstimated that our human brain has a memory capacity of around 1000 terabytes. The human brain is a relatively slow electro-chemical, carbon based, thinking machine. The computer is a super-fast electronic, silicon based, computing device. The computer wins hands-down at computing speed. And yet, the cauliflower shaped, wetware ball we call our brain has a big advantage over the electronic computer. Each single brain cell or neuron has a synaptic connection that allows it to connect with and network about 10,000 other brain cells. It's almost like you have a multitude of little internets all working together within your skull. The total connectivity within the brain has a capacity somewhere in the vicinity of trillions of possible connections. This connectivity makes any super-computer look like a laughable toy in comparison. Of course the computer has a big advantage in speed, and you can link additional silicon chips together to increase its storage. How do humans stack up against the computer? The computer needs human intervention to supply its power and turn it on. Once someone turns the power on; they will still need to tell this silicon based dummy what, where, when, and how to do it. The computer cannot make a single decision without you hitting the power button and someone giving it a long list of written instructions. We call these step by step instructions a computer program. Once the computer is programmed; it needs someone to supply data for it to manipulate, so that it can spit out an answer that some human is looking for. Just as a car has no idea of where it's going, the computer is unaware of what is happening. Watson the famed IBM computer that won the TV Jeopardy contest did not know that it was in a contest and it had no idea that it won. Without directions from the human brain; neither the car, nor Watson would know what the hell they're doing. Here's the whole point of this computer verses brain comparison. You can be sure that you have a magnificent brain. Your intellect puts you light years beyond the computer. You are gifted with the human brain; the most powerful creative intelligent force that has ever appeared on planet earth. For all we know it's possible that no greater marvel of intelligence has appeared anywhere else in the entire universe. With this kind of brainpower in your possession there should be no doubt that you have brilliant undiscovered capabilities and almost unimaginable potential.

Understanding the brains immense capability should fill you with confidence. You can direct this power to your advantage. This is something you can believe in. To increase your conviction, listen to the words of the great Napoleon Hill "Whatever the mind of man can conceive and believe the mind of man can achieve." What can activate you and your brainpower? All you need is grand vision for your life and the desire to act on it. Immediately get started because the best is yet to come.

Chapter 11
Inevitable Outcome

"I write for the same reason I breathe - because if I didn't, I would die."

Isaac Asimov

The prolific science fiction writer Isaac Asimov was also a professor of biochemistry at Boston University. His writing career was his first love and he turned out and published hundreds of books. Asimov said he felt compelled to write because he enjoyed it so much. Once in a conversation with a friend he related that when it was time to take his family on vacation; his stomach would become queasy. He said this was because he knew he would have to interrupt his writing routine. While he was on vacation he would still find a way to write. On vacation he would often tackle a subject different than his usual writing of science fiction. On one of his vacations he even wrote a book on jokes and humor. At one time he was asked to join a group of authors who were operating a correspondence course on writing for novice writers. It was aimed to help aspiring writers who wanted guidance and advice from established writers. The authors running this school had created a list of recommended general rules for all writers. One of the rules stated that a writer had to make a firm commitment to writing for at least an hour a day 5 days a week. Asimov said he could not support that rule, because he felt exactly the opposite way about writing. Isaac Asimov declared that he had to discipline himself to stop writing. This was a man obsessed with writing because it gave him great pleasure. He once said: *"If my doctor told me I had only six minutes to live, I wouldn't brood. I'd type a little faster."*

Asimov is a man who surely found his purpose in life. It is doubtful that most people would want to be so devoted to just one thing. The average person sees a balanced life as a more rewarding way to live. But imagine if you catch a little of this man's fire for whatever you are seeking in life. You would surely become an accomplished, and prosperous expert. How can that be done you ask? I see great possibilities for you if you make a commitment to your chosen quest. Sometimes it helps to ask yourself, am I working on my highest priority? Once committed totally to an activity you will usually start enjoying what you're doing. An urge from within compels you to repeat the activity again and again, and it could become an enjoyable habit. The Unrelenting Little Efforts over time will help turn wishes into reality.

Chapter 12
The Game of Life

"Deep within man dwell those slumbering powers; powers that would astonish him, that he never dreamed of possessing; forces that would revolutionize his life if aroused and put into action."

Orison Swett Marden

Professor B.F. Skinner spent a lifetime as a behavioral psychologist studying why we do what we do. He boiled it down to two driving forces, pain and pleasure. Of course the carrot and stick notion existed long before Skinner was born, and it's common knowledge that we avoid pain and seek pleasure. Skinner looked deeper suspecting that pain and pleasure influenced our actions beyond our understanding. His scientific study illuminated the powerful control these twin forces exert in our everyday lives. Animal learning experiments were conducted, and lab animals were put into what became known as the Skinner Box. Along with the animals the box contained food and an apparatus to generate mild electrical shock, simulating pain and pleasure. These components served as tools to coax certain behaviors. Through repetitive pain-pleasure stimulus; lab rats, pigeons and other animals developed habitual behaviors called conditioning. These experiments were designed to discover if people also became conditioned from normal stimulus in their environment.

It is well known that another noted scientist, Pavlov carried out similar behavioral research with dogs. His highly publicized experiment had dogs salivating at the ringing of a bell because the dogs expected to receive food anytime the bell started ringing. Skinner and Pavlov seem to be saying that much of what we do is not controlled by rational choice, but by the feelings of the moment. This research suggests that our choices are often unwise, we act with little forethought as we opt to gain instant gratification. This information is important because our choices are largely responsible for our health, happiness, and success. This is all worth exploring because if we are being conditioned, we want it to be for success and not failure.

Throughout the ages people with knowledge have had more advantages in life than others who were less informed. The most sought-after knowledge has resided in the fields of business, finance, medicine, technology, etc. The study of behavior is not thought of as a way to prosper in the world, but could it be the most advantageous way?

Behavioral scientists have been telling us what they've discovered, but we remain uninterested. They've pointed out that when we make our everyday decisions, we're caught in a tug of war that pulls at us to either avoid pain or gain pleasure. This conflict causes our vision to be blurred, and we don't see clearly the choice that would have made our life better tomorrow. Instead, we choose instant satisfaction to avoid a small hurt or enjoy a small treat. This impulsive choosing of easy but unwise choices keeps us from reaching the sunny days we all desire. We don't really need science to make us aware that the lure of instant pleasure causes us to make decisions that are losers, and we instinctively know the more difficult decision would have given us a brighter future. So how can we take control and make better choices so that we can have the best life possible? We need to start by convincing ourselves of the great things we can accomplish by making a few more intelligent choices. If we only made one wise choice a day, how many would that be in a year? Deep inside we know it is possible to design the future we want, simply because we have the power to choose. Understand that even tiny decisions are opportunities for a better life. This is an internal battle so we'll play a game where we must make the very best choice to win at this game of life. We know that difficult choices are often the best choices over the long run. So we should boldly make the best choice. Know that there will be times when we are feeling tremendous pressure to take the easy way out. What can we do at a time when we feel weak?

The advice I'm about to give you should only be practiced in private, you don't want people thinking you're crazy. Self-talk might help you and saying your desired purpose out loud might give you some courage and determination. Three examples follow. "I challenge myself to do the difficult thing!" "I will not be denied!" "I'm a winner, and I intend to win at this game of life!" A vocal or mental pep-talk like this can do the trick, and help you boldly make the right positive choice. When you act bravely you are also developing your will, and a strong will gives you a big advantage in dealing with life's challenges. Imagine people saying this to you: "You have a will of iron." Of course, taking a different approach might also work. You could dramatically yell out "I'm not going to mess my whole life up by giving in to this (you fill in the blank.)

Imagination can fire up your desire to live better. See yourself living and enjoying the most desirable life you can dream up. Thinking of what you want can inspire you to gain control and make good choices. You see yourself eating healthy, spending wisely, exercising daily, doing all the things you know will lead to an improved lifestyle. You see in advance your tomorrows being the absolute best. You know that others have done this and so can you. Choose correctly and you will be rewarded with improved health, finances, fitness, and all the things that can make life more enjoyable. A happy life is what we're all looking for and making one good choice after another can turn your life into a delightful adventure.

Chapter 13
Struggle

"I hated every minute of training, but I said, Don't quit. Suffer now and live the rest of your life as a champion."

Muhammad Ali

Struggle has shaped the entire development of mankind, civilization, and individuals. Human striving has taken mankind from the cave to the moon. One of the greatest struggles that ever occurred was a race for victory that occurred during World War II. Three countries at war became aware that an ultimate destructive weapon might just be possible. The leaders of these countries were convinced that the first country to develop this weapon could achieve military superiority and certain victory. The race was on, and the whole world was about to be changed because of Einstein's Theory of Relativity. The theory's equation $E=MC2$ postulated that mass and energy were equal, and that mass could be converted to energy. Physicists calculated that if the basic unit of matter, the atom, could be split it would release enormous energy. The math indicated that 1 ounce of matter (about the weight of a AA battery) would yield the equivalent energy of 600,000 tons of TNT. To weapon makers this meant that they could use a tiny amount of material to create a relatively small, deliverable, and enormously powerful bomb. The United States and allies were at war with Germany, and Japan. These three major nations were all competing to develop this super weapon. In 1939 the United States made a commitment to be the first country to build the atom bomb. The decision resulted in the creation of a top secret mission called the Manhattan Project. It involved over 100,000 people all struggling to be first to develop this ultimate weapon of war. This struggle paid off when the United States won the race, dropped the bomb, and accelerated an end to World War II. Many nations came to believe that this devastating bomb would make war unthinkable, and the result would be an end to all wars. This was wishful thinking; we know war continues to plague mankind to this day. This new reality only made clear that no country wants to be faced with demands made under threat of annihilation. Consequently, not long after the first mushroom cloud appeared, other nations became members of this exclusive club with the potential to destroy the planet. Man's efforts always lead to bigger, stronger, faster, and more powerful things. Thus, an even more destructive bomb was created. The hydrogen bomb also converted matter to energy, not by splitting the atom, but by fusing atoms together. Now the human race is involved in the ultimate struggle, we must prevent mankind from self-extinction. Though we are on the cusp of apocalypse; most nations are rational. They subscribe to a belief in 'mutually assured destruction' which so far has kept us from destroying the world. War continues, but the ultimate weapon is in hibernation, and has not been used since World War II. The Manhattan Project is an example of the awesome power of group struggle for survival. As individuals we also struggle for survival, it's our primary instinct. The overwhelming desire to keep on living is a constant pulse within every sane human. We are fragile creatures; we can survive for only 3 minutes without oxygen, 3 days without water, and 3 weeks without food. We are programmed by nature to be either struggling for the necessities of life, or shelter from harm. With the right thinking and motivation, we can be in harmony with our survival instinct. This book is dedicated to give you that winning edge. We can develop daily habits that will make us grow, stimulated by the challenges we face. When we are winning life's battles, we feel happy. If our daily efforts are leading to growth, in any area we consider important, we feel pleasure. If our efforts ultimately lead to accomplishment, that's wonderful, and we feel joy. This type of daily progress can generate a constant feeling of well-being and can become habit forming. When we've established a success habit we will still face challenges, but now we're free to focus on improving some other aspect of our life. Properly directed struggle, on a regular basis, make both the mind and body stronger. *"Where there is no struggle, there is no strength."* Oprah Winfrey

Struggle leads to progress and when we are making progress, we are living life to the full, and to paraphrase Muhammad Ali: *"After successful struggle we can live the rest of life as a champion."*

Chapter 14
Thinking

"Every man builds his world in his own image. He has the power to choose, but no power to escape the necessity of choice."

Ayn Rand

By the roll of the dice you are a fortunate person. Over a billion of your fellow humans live in the underdeveloped world in abject poverty, with little chance of escaping. The primary reason; they are illiterate. They cannot tap into the abundance of human intelligent thought that has been captured in print for hundreds of years. Around 1454 Gutenberg's printing press first appeared, and thus began a major advancement in man's progress. This was an advancement as great if not greater than today's internet. For the first time in history information became inexpensive, transportable, and easily accessed by large numbers of people. It was truly the first time information became mobile. This same information is now super-mobile, because it can be delivered wirelessly to advanced parts of the world. Just in time, because glacially slow is the progress being made to reach and educate the billions who now live in ignorance of this vast knowledge that man has accumulated. This information is so powerful that it has raised everyone in the literate world up to incredible wealth; when compared with a thousand years ago. Even today, American's living in poverty are prosperous in relation to the poor now living in the under-developed world.

We are surrounded by the thoughts of creative people we've never met. We rarely link thought to the objects surrounding us, yet every manmade object in our material world first existed in the intangible vapor of thought. Just glance around wherever you are at this moment. You're seeing the images of man's thinking reproduced in every manufactured object. Our existence has been enhanced by the thoughts of man in every conceivable way. We have brought innovation and improvement to the way we grow our food, heal our bodies, and sanitize our drinking water. Physically we are weaklings when compared to other creatures. We are no match for the elephant, tiger, grizzly bear etc. Man rules the animal world because our superior thoughts make up for any physical deficiency. The thoughts of man have made us the most powerful creatures on this planet. We can lift, push, and sprint far beyond any beast of burden. We've also enhanced our brain power because we've created computers. These computers help us process information at speeds far beyond that of our biological brain. We can now transport ourselves and our supplies; anywhere on planet earth and beyond. There can be no doubt, all humans are creators, and we have the power to bring our thoughts into reality. We must be careful and think civilized thoughts because our thoughts will replicate and become real. Dissatisfaction brings out the genius in man, and because he can think he can change his world. Our thinking reproduces itself, through our actions, so it behooves us to think elevated thoughts. I have been unable to find a quote I once heard so I will paraphrase it: "*From the same material one man builds a grotto; another a castle.*" Because you have this power, the power to think, you can create the best life possible for you.

Chapter 15
Vision Power

You are in possession of one of the great marvels of this universe. A force so powerful that it protects you from harm and gets you the things you want and need. An entity so clever and reliable that at your direction it can work out plans for your future. We can only be talking about your brain. Consciously and subconsciously this wizard helps to make your life easier. It puts you on autopilot as you dress, groom, and drive.

I doubt you think much about how your great mind has served you, we all take such miracles for granted. Imagine if you were able to uncover a more effective method of harnessing your brain power by understanding how it operates. With that knowledge you would likely be able to make even greater progress. You could take more direct control of your life.

Truly this is possible; you can up your level of influence to have a more rewarding life. The principle is simple, and you already have a working knowledge of it. The system works unconsciously in the background of your mind. You are unaware of it, but it is always in operation. You have no reason to pay attention because the system works. You don't need to know exactly how a doorbell, or a car engine works, as long as they are working. But if you have knowledge of how your brain works it means that you can have greater influence in directing it to do your bidding. Also, you can gain more skill at navigating through life. If you already know how to do it, you can skip over this chapter, if you'd like to know more I encourage you to keep reading.

This vital control you need can be found in the area of the brain devoted to vision. It is the largest segment of our brain, and it works directly to interpret what our eyes see. It does much more than just give us sight. We don't need to know the exact function or inner workings of the brain in order to gain the control we are looking for. We are not trying to become brain surgeons, but we should educate ourselves as to the nomenclature of the two major parts for informational purposes. They are the Occipital Lobe and the Visual Cortex. Together they serve in the act of seeing, and in the ability to conjure up mental visions past, present, and future.

It works like this: You have an ultra-clear fixed vision of what you want, or where you want to go. If the vision is important to you, it has persistence, it is not easily overridden by other visions.

I want to give you a simple example, and I may have used this example elsewhere in this book. It's the best way I know how to make this point. When you are driving your car you keep your mind on one simple thought (It's a vision of) your destination. If you were always changing your mind about where your headed, you would never get anywhere. Out of sight, out of mind, has brought many success stories to a premature end.

Here is another way of looking at it. When you have a clear, fixed, and desirable vision you will be drawn to that vision. It is not so easy to hold fast to a vision; life is full of distractions. If I tell you not to think about a pink elephant; I have just disrupted other visions in your head. You had to make room for my pink elephant. By the way! I told you not to think about the pink elephant!

This silly example indicates how difficult it is to hold fast to a vision, it requires a little effort. Putting your vision in writing will help.

As an experiment to test this power of vision; try this: Take a moment and envision some very simple task you want to perform today. Make an effort to hold the vision of that simple act. Keep holding, and soon you can't help but feel the power of a compelling force driving you to satisfy that vision. This is the way your mind works. A clear vision can bring both small and big changes into your life. Monumental achievements require an absolute commitment to lock that vision into your inner eye.

Now you have the key to one of your vital controls: Vision Power. Now it's up to you to choose the visions that will take you where you want to go. Direct your vision to an exciting dream life and your super powerful brain will work on that vision and get you moving so you can live on the easy street you visualized.

Chapter 16
Change The Channel

"Our life always expresses the result of our dominant thoughts."

Soren Kierkegaard

Reading only this chapter just might give you an ability that you didn't know you had. This one ability can reduce much daily aggravation, and annoyance. This is something easy to do, and it works, and it will make you happier.

I'm getting ahead of myself so let me explain what I'm referring to. It's a curious thing that most people entertain whatever thought pops into their head. They dwell on it even when the thought has no useful purpose, and it carries with it the feeling of discontent. Such thoughts push out tranquility and happiness. Let me be clear I'm only talking about trivial thoughts, and not important thoughts about actions you must take to solve some problem you are facing. Procrastination can have an effect on your mind anytime you avoid some necessary but painful activity. Other chapters in this book will help you 'kill that monster.'

We are shining the spotlight on nonproductive downer thoughts. These upsetting thoughts are like rain drops, no one can avoid them. Some examples: You've just heard a news story that disturbs you. It does not affect your life, and there is nothing you can do to change the situation, but you let it upset you. Think this instead, I can't control what is happing in the whole wide world, but I have enormous influence in my own little world.

Another example. You think back to a mistake that you made years ago (or 10 minutes ago). You know you can't change the past, and yet it puts you in gloomy mood. Replace that thought with some happy thought about what you are looking forward to.

It happens to everyone; out of nowhere upsetting thoughts come down from above like space invaders trying to enter your head. Now imagine that you can shoot them down, before they land and upset you. It can be done; let me suggest a technique that will help you take control. Master this technique and you will develop the ability to protect yourself from the invasion of discouraging thoughts. The first thing you need to understand is that these thoughts will try to sneak by you. They don't want you to discover them until they have spoiled your good mood. If you're starting to feel down; that sounds the alarm. You can be sure one of these gloomy thoughts has entered into your mind.

What to do. It's simple. Change the Channel! Just as you change the TV channel when you don't like what's on. You can do this immediately by thinking of a more pleasant thought. You absolutely have the power to choose one thought over another. There is always something in your life that's going right. Reflect on it. Or pull up a thought from the abundant bin of things you should be grateful for. There are a vast number of items in your inventory of blessings that can pick up your mood if you dwell on them.

When you think an uplifting thought it will block out the depressing thought and keep it from taking hold.

Change the Channel it's a simple game that you can win. Just think, if you can become skillful at this game; you could become the world champion of positive thinkers. Like every skill in life, it will take a little practice to do this on a consistent basis. Good ideas are great but unless they play an active part in your life, they're useless.

If you like this idea, give it a try and you'll find out that you are in control of you. To help you be a winner at this game, I've created a memory aid that will help you keep practicing until you've mastered this skill. Grab your remote and put a rubber band around it. Use this visual cue to remind you to 'Change the Channel' whenever the bad thought alarm goes off. You might want to change this visual cue often, because we all tend to ignore the ordinary everyday cues we see all the time. Use a piece of tape or some other marker on the remote so that this idea will stay fresh in your mind. Develop this skill and you will be able to replace a discouraging thought with an uplifting thought. Your ultimate reward will be immunity from trivial, gloomy thoughts. Our mood is controlled by our thoughts, but we can decide which thoughts we will hold in our mind. Also, we eventually start moving in the direction of what we are thinking about, so you want to be moving to a brighter future. You can take control of your happiness now because you know how to 'Change the Channel.'

Chapter 17
Want

"Know what you want to do, hold the thought firmly, and do every day what should be done, and every sunset will see you that much nearer to your goal."

Elbert Hubbard

The single-minded intention of this book is to inspire, convince, and help you get what you want from life. Want is a simple word, and yet want is the driving force in your life. This little word has had more effect on your life than any other in your vocabulary. Much of what you've obtained in life is mostly the result of your past wants. You do this all the time when you decide what you want to do and where you want to go. Destinations, possessions, skills, careers, everything starts with the want button. It's that simple, you want, you act, and with a little persistence you get the thing you want. It happens over and over in your life, and I guarantee it will happen again today.

Let's be clear, we're not talking about wishes or preferences. It's easy to confuse preferences with wants. I believe that everyone would prefer to be physically fit, but only those who want fitness enough to act will reach that desired condition. Little wants easily fade away and die, it happens all the time.

When you truly want something it's almost certain you

will act, and you will get it. Let me define exactly what I mean by the term want with the following example. If you received a heart transplant, it would require taking exact quantities of medication, at specific times, to prevent rejection. Your want would be so strong that you would be determined to follow through. Have no doubt if your want is overwhelming it will give you an unrelenting will to win. Arnold Palmer expressed his thoughts on this subject. "Winning isn't everything, but wanting it is."

This book contains ideas to realize everything you've ever wanted. Ideas that will help you gain confidence and pump up your want power. You need only to develop a crystal clear, fixed vision of what you urgently desire. It must be singular, just one thing at a time. When your want power is absolute, you will form the attitude of a doer: "I can do it, and I will do it." In this frame of mind, you'll be able to meet any challenge. You're in control, you're holding the steering wheel, and you can drive straight to success. Hit the accelerator by taking action, and now you're happily pursuing whatever you want.

Chapter 18
Stress and Eustress

"It's not stress that kills us; it is our reaction to it."

Hans Selye

Dr. Hans Selye began his study on stress in 1936 and became so fascinated with what he learned that he decided to devote his entire career to the subject. Dr. Selye came to this conclusion from his years of study. "Adapting the right attitude can convert a negative stress into a positive one." He coined the word eustress, which means a form of stress that promotes a favorable effect on health, motivation, performance, and well-being. We all know that negative stress can make our life miserable and have a detrimental effect on our health. Being able to handle stress is a useful skill to have as it gives you the best chance for good health and an untroubled mind. When stress is under control you feel calm, and you sleep like a baby. Imagine being able to counter negative stress by flipping the switch over to its positive counterpart. If you learn to do this, you can experience all the benefits of eustress as described above. In this chapter I will challenge you to learn how you can have the upper hand when stressful situations arise. With this knowledge you will have less anguish, and more enthusiasm for life.

We've all experienced moments where we felt wonderful and we live to experience those feelings again. Believe it or not, those happy times were not stress free. You were experiencing the positive stress that Dr. Selye illuminated in his studies. Those stirring feelings we enjoy come from thoughts and actions that create powerful uplifting emotions. Life is always in a state of flux, a never-ending mixture of up and down moments. The trick is to convert or eliminate as much of the negative pressure as possible. Let's look at how we can be in control of stress and not vice-versa.

Procrastination might head the list of things that rob us of tranquility. How do we feel when we have a problem or distasteful duty hanging over our head? Miserable, and we all know that running away from it will keep us in a depressed mood. Yet often we choose to live in this self-imposed misery. Fear immobilizes us. Yet on the other side of fear, we know is the relief we crave. Once the difficulty is over, we can relax and start enjoying life again, but we're frozen in time. In a sense we've tricked ourselves into inaction. Let's see if we can trick our way out.

Let's start by doing something super easy. You can plant a little action seed. How? Simply write down the easiest thing you can think of to take a small nibble out of the frighting task before you. Once this little seed has been planted on paper you will start to feel motivated. Next, you'll be amazed at how this tiny little action seed you planted blossoms, and incredibly it spurs you into action. The simple act of writing a 'to do' is often all it takes for you to go forward. You write it down, it gets you moving, and best of all your stress is converted into a feeling of exhilaration. If this idea works for you great, but if it is not a strategy that appeals to you lets try a more direct approach.

We've all been in situations that make us feel like we're a trapped animal. We must decide or do something we desperately would like to avoid. Spring loose from this trap by taking just one simple step to address the thing tormenting you. When you act, almost instantaneously the burden lifts. You have the feeling you can handle it and do even more. It's a happy feeling. Strange how you dreaded even the thought of doing anything, but action has lifted your mood, and now you feel wonderful. When you work up the courage to act, you've set yourself free. Action releases the stress and turn it into the energy you need to do what you have to do. There is another benefit, you'll remember how you did it and be armed for the future. If you desire to live a more stress-free life, it comes at a cost, and action is the price you must pay for such luxury. The great insurance tycoon W. Clement Stone stated it simply: "Thinking will not overcome fear, but action will."

Getting into action is always the solution for converting negative stress into positive energy. When you win out over stress, it's like the sun just came out, and you feel warm and happy all over.

Chapter 19
Singularity

"We succeed only as we identify in life, or in war, or in anything else, a single overriding objective, and make all other considerations bend to that one objective."

Dwight D. Eisenhower

In the world of physics Singularity is a momentous occurrence. It describes the existence an infinitesimal unit of energy, smaller than the atom. According to the Big Bang Theory of the Universe, this tiny dot of energy exploded and expanded at incredible speed, creating the massive universe in which we now live.

In the domain of computer science, Singularity theoretically predicts a frightening time. It anticipates when artificial intelligence reaches equivalence and eventually exceeds human intelligence, robots become sentient, and humans possibly lose control.

Both theories, are yet to be proven. The Singularity we are going to discuss has been proven. It is also momentous because it's powerful enough to change and expand your world. It is best described in the words of Carl von Clausewitz: *"Pursue one great decisive aim with force and determination."*

Singularity is the decision to isolate and act upon one single objective. When something is truly important in your life, you block out, at least temporarily, all other objectives. It's been said that if you are working on more than one priority, you have no priority. That may be a little extreme, but to accomplish things you must be focused and eliminate distractions. If low priorities are competing for your attention, it will be difficult for you to accomplish much. With a single-minded dedication to one purpose, you will advance, you will make progress, and you will succeed.

If you have a magnificent obsession that will take a lifetime to complete, it will require an intense focus taking small steps one by one on the stairway to success. Each milestone reached will give you confidence and intensify your desire, until you feel that the objective is almost in your grasp. With this type of conviction, you will not stop until you are rewarded. This is what President Franklin D. Roosevelt had to say on this subject: "Happiness lies in the joy of achievement and the thrill of creative effort."

Some might worry that such an obsession would lead to an unbalanced life. The much bigger danger is that you will drown in a swirl of trivial activities. With a fixed purpose, leading to significant accomplishments, you will take your place in the winner's circle. Singularity is the superhighway you travel to get to your destiny. When you arrive, you'll feel the special pride and joy of those who have achieved their dreams.

Chapter 20
Focus

"Concentrate all your thoughts upon the work at hand. The sun's rays do not burn until brought to a focus."

Alexander Graham Bell

I remember as a young boy I had a simple magnifying glass and I held it over dry leaves, in less than a minute the leaves burst into flames. Without pinpointing the sun's rays how long would the sun have to shine before those leaves caught fire? Nature had given me my first demonstration on the power of focus. This is a discovery everyone should make because we all have power and when it is focused we can do all sorts of marvelous things. Focusing can make what seems impossible possible. This intensity of power helps you remove obstacles, achieve goals, learn new skills and do so much more. Focus is not a difficult to understand magic; you simply keep your mind on a task that you are committed to completing. It is the force you need to get things done. It's basic, all you have to do is isolate, focus, and finish. Winners and great achievers are simply people who have focused on mastering a certain subject or performance. For instance, if you're devoted to fitness your resulting actions will keep you on course to be fit. Focusing on trivial activities can keep a person amused, but it is unlikely to lead to a satisfying life experience. An uplifting way of living comes from centering on high priority activities. Actions dedicated to keep us growing mentally, physically, and financially so we can have a more fulfilling life.

Determination is needed to stay focused on important activities because distractions are everywhere. Once off course, you can drown in a sea of minutia. You can rescue yourself, if you come to the realization that you are wasting your most valuable resource, time. When this happens, you can quickly go back and focus on what is most important to you. Now, you hold fast to your true priority and fight off any further diversions.

No, it is not all that easy to stay focused. Daily life is challenging for everyone, it never stops interrupting with some demand to grab our attention. If you have isolated a sacred period of time for the central thing you are engaged in, you are less likely to lose focus. Those who respond to every disruption will accomplish little, other than staying alive. When you focus you have the power to shape things in your own little world, forming them to match your wishes for a better life.

Many people would jump at the chance to have the power of focus working for them, but not at the expense of giving up their but easygoing lifestyle. They know life for them would be just marvelous if only there were a pill you could take to remedy a lack of focus. Unfortunately, no such pill exists. The cure can only be found when you decide that you deserve a better life, and you're willing to awaken the giant within you, called focus.

Sometimes fear or anger is all the motivation a person needs to focus and get into action. You can make big ideas reachable, by focusing on doing small things well.

When you focus, you create an expectant eagerness, and a belief that you can do the thing you've decided to do.

Does it work? Of course, all your power is brought to bear on the task at hand, and success is close to certainty. With focus you are on the road to mastery, you become convinced that the thing can and will be done. U.S Investing Champion, Mark Minervini, put it this way: *"When you truly commit to something you have no alternative but success."*

From the study of physics, we know that normal light scatters photons far and wide with zero effect on solid objects. However, once you focus those photons you create a laser beam which can cut through a block of steel. This analogy is as close as you can get to what happens when you focus your energy, it is released and directed on exactly what you have in mind. It creates a feeling that it is impossible to fail. Finally, after holding fast you are elated with the outcome. You sit back and reflect on how you worked diligently with a laser like focus and it has brought what you envisioned into reality. Now you are convinced: Isolate, focus, and finish it's a sure-fire formula for success.

Chapter 21
Genie in the Bottle

"My goal is to create a metaphor that changes our reality by charming people into considering their world in a different way."

Chuck Palahniuk

One of the most beloved stories of all time is the story of the genie in the bottle. As you remember if you rub the bottle, you free the genie, and ask that your fondest wish be granted. The genie grants your wish. This story has endured for a lifetime because we would all like to find a way to get our wishes granted. It's a fairy tale of course but imagine if in the real world such a force existed. It does, and you've been in contact with the genie many times, and all your wishes have come true. Action was your genie. You acted and voila what you wished for appeared. Your story is real, not fantasy, you acted, and you got what you wanted. Just like the genie you have the power to make things happen. Now the genie is out of the bottle, you know your true ability to get what you desire. I used the metaphor of the genie to show the power of action. Everywhere you look you will see marvels of man's creative powers expressed as a result of action. The Pyramids, Landing on the Moon, Taj Mahal, Jet Flights Around the World, Great Wall of China, everywhere you look you see spectacular ideas

brought to life by the power of action. *"Action is the foundational key to all success."* Pablo Picasso
We are all truly gifted, we have the power to bring our thoughts into reality. Meaning that everyone can improve their life and make it as beautiful as they can imagine. So why doesn't everyone act? Thoughts of failure are always lurking in our mind. Visions of failure make us weak and stop us from taking the action that would delight us. Thoughts of success or failure are not real. They are thoughts they do not exist in the real world.

The difference is this; thoughts of failure, commonly referred to as negative thoughts, cause us to imagine all sorts of frightening difficulties in our way. Ominous visions lay ahead, people, places, and things all out to bring us down and make us miserable. Expecting failure or trouble makes us feel weak and tired with no desire to act. Everything we want is down the road of success, but we don't have the courage to act and step forward. Overwhelmed with negativity we are immobilized. This type of thinking would keep the genie himself from ever wanting to escape the bottle.
Fortunately, we also have the ability to think positive thoughts. Thoughts of success stimulate our desire to act. Often just jumping into action will change our thoughts into uplifting expectations. Once these thoughts kick in you have more energy, you're ready to tackle obstacles that might appear. You are excited about the reward you're seeking and that keeps you going. We're all on a journey through this life, and the wonderful thing is we can choose to think success or failure. When you think success it's like rubbing the bottle to release the genie, you are about to make your wishes come true. While on your journey be encouraged

from the words of Michelangelo: "*Great works come to life by steadily chipping away.*" Your great life can come into reality, because you've been given the power to choose, think, and act. Imagine how fabulous it's going to be once you arrive.

Chapter 22
One Desire

*"The first step to getting the things you want out of life
is this: Decide what you want"*

Ben Stein

Does your mind swirl with visions of countless things
that you hope for? Pick one! What just happened?
You've singled out your uppermost wish and put a spotlight on it, conflicting desires fade away. By doing this
you've set forces in motion that can propel you forward.
You're more likely to act when single-minded in your
desire. When you focus on one thing, your power is no
longer scattered. You've uncomplicated your life. What
was difficult is now easy, because you've singled out
what is important to you. When you imagine being successful you feel the pleasure in advance. Your expectation will drive you on to seek the thing you desire. With
unrelenting action, you will not be denied the vision
you're in search of. When totally focused in this way
you have the absolute best chance to achieve whatever it
is that you want. Even if all your skills are not up to par
you will gain competence as you plow forward. When
you were a baby you experienced this type of motivation, you wanted to walk and now it's a permanent part
of your skill set. This is the way we accomplish things.
The founder of Virgin Airlines Richard Branson de-

scribes it this way. *"You don't learn to walk by following rules. You learn by doing, and by falling over"* It's a new day! Zero in on that one thing that excites you. Decide to go after it now. Only doubt can stop you from gaining your true desire. William Shakespeare's good advice has been heeded for over 400 years: *"Our doubts are traitors, and make us lose the good we oft might win, by fearing to attempt."* When you're totally committed to one pursuit it will be yours. Once you've succeeded, you'll find satisfaction is short lived. Soon you'll be chasing a new dream. In case you need inspiration take heart from another dream chaser. Elon Musk, the CEO of Tesla Motors, SpaceX, and Solar City is making plans to go to Mars.

Chapter 23
New Exhilarating Heights

"It is not knowledge, but the act of learning, not possession but the act of getting there, which grants the greatest enjoyment."

Carl Friedrich Gauss

At this moment in time anyone with a desire to learn has an advantage unequaled in recorded history. Instant access to knowledge of limitless subjects has been achieved. The internet is at your fingertips. Everyone alive today has access to more information than all the brilliant scholars who lived prior to this modern era. Can you imagine what Michelangelo or Einstein could have achieved if they had access to the internet's fountain of knowledge?

There was one other time in history, back before Columbus discovered America, when a powerful breakthrough in learning occurred. It was a giant leap forward for mankind and it happened in 1454. Gutenberg's printing press made it easy to copy, reproduce. and deliver information. This evolution made knowledge widely accessible in the form of relatively inexpensive books. It's difficult to measure the exact impact this distribution of knowledge had on the human condition, but surely it was the precursor to today's internet.

We know this, before the printing press very few people

had access to recorded knowledge. Only subjects deemed worthy were being recorded, and it was a slow process to capture knowledge. Monks were producing handwritten books. These books remained in one place, and they could only be read by people of a certain status like scholars. For the first time in history information was available to the masses. The number of subjects that could be studied multiplied and new discoveries were unveiled and shared by entire populations. Living standards improved as progress through learning spread around the world. Everything we've achieved since was built on the Gutenberg transformation.

We are now light years beyond the printing press, the internet is in the palm of your hand. Every subject imaginable is instantaneously available, transmitted wirelessly, displayed in print, graphs, pictures, voice, and video. When we hit a problem, the internet is our first choice to solve it. Late one night, my son could not get his car out of park. He was about to have the car towed, but first he searched the internet on his smart phone. Sure enough, this was a common problem. A sensor in the brake pedal was not working. The brakes were not damaged, but a safety sensor was not working. There was no signal being sent to indicate that the brake pedal was depressed. The shift lever could not be moved to drive until that signal was received. Fortunately, his smart phone indicated that an override switch was close at hand. He flipped the switch, drove home and had the defective sensor replaced the next day. This type of problem solving is a blessing, but it's almost insignificant when we look at total power of the internet. Researching any subject on the internet is so easy that we no longer go to encyclopedias or libraries for answers. The potential for education on the internet is unlimited. Every culture in the world believes in the necessity of education, and teaching our children is as natural as feeding them. During the current pandemic online education helped to make up for lost classroom time as schools were shut down. Many students complained that they could not learn as well online as they could in class. Of course, this is true, online learning requires a distraction free environment, and a little discipline. Also, it is meant to be a supplement and not a replacement for schoolhouse learning. Online you lose the social interaction, comradery, and personalized instruction necessary for complete learning. Remote education will continue to improve, and currently it is being integrated with classroom education at every level from the university down to kindergarten. This is a good thing because there can be no doubt everyone will need to know how to navigate and use the internet as a learning tool, now and even more so in the future. Creative people, educators, video game developers, and others are looking for ways to make on-line learning easier, more engaging, and fun. Possibly in time it will become the preferred way to learn and master certain difficult subjects. There is no question that the internet has helped to advance man's knowledge, and that will continue to accelerate making the world a better place. Everyone can observe that in highly educated societies, poverty declines, and prosperity increases. We know that the internet can spread knowledge quickly throughout the world, hopefully reaching the underprivileged populations. For all these reasons the internet is destined to play an escalating role in the education of all seven billion-plus people on this planet.

Knowledge is exploding and changing so fast that no one can keep up. The internet can serve as somewhat of an equalizer. I know Benjamin Franklin would have loved the internet, he said this: *"Tell me and I forget. Teach me and I remember. Involve me and I learn."* The magnificence of the internet is that it will involve you, in fact it will act as your personal tutor. Take advantage, the internet is a force multiplier for your magnificent brain. This is the opportunity of our lifetime, and it can take your life to exhilarating heights.

Chapter 24
Your Future

"Your life will be no better than the plans you make, and the actions you take. You are the architect and builder of your own life, fortune and destiny."

Alfred A. Montapert

Did you know that you could predict your future? Your mind is always taking you into the future. We are always thinking ahead anticipating how to get what we want and how to avoid what we don't want. Before you rode your first bike or drove your first car it played out in your mind. Your thoughts have brought you to where you are now, and your thoughts will take you to where you're going to be. Neuroscientists tell us that our neocortex, which makes up 80% of our brain, is focused on the future. It anticipates what our next step should be. Without thinking about the future, our outlook is cloudy, and we wander aimlessly like an untethered rowboat in a choppy sea. Buddha expressed this clearly when he wrote: "What we are today comes from our thoughts of yesterday, and our present thoughts build our life of tomorrow. Our life is the creation of our mind." It makes sense to plan one's life. Planning can define the most desirable life wanted and create the roadmap we need to get there. With a plan we clarify our dreams and lay out the steps needed to go where we want to go and obtain the things we desire. It is very difficult if not impossible to plan out all the steps, however, if we take the first step the next step will become clear and on and on. Will there be detours, of course but at least we know where we're going. We always have the option to wing it and go where life takes us. Without a plan it's doubtful we will live our dream life, and possibly we'd be living in a nightmare we never contemplated. Evidence is abundant from every field that planning is an effective tool. An architect is a planner who defines exactly what is to be created before it is brought into existence. The concept is drawn up as a blueprint and it becomes the plan builders will follow. The final result materializes to match the architect's vision. No building, missile, computer or battleship has ever been built without a detailed plan. Without a doubt these monuments of man's ingenuity are important. They provide convenience and protection for people. It seems obvious that planning is necessary for all our creations. It makes sense that a person's life is important and deserving of a plan.

Sports preparation is another example of just how important planning is. Professional Boxing, Football, Soccer, and Basketball coaches are paid a lot of money to design winning strategies. They spend most of their time planning. All planners know that no plan ever works out perfectly. Mike Tyson famously said: "Everyone has a plan 'till they get punched in the mouth." It's true plans don't always work out and planners are always changing the plan to get it right. When coaches are not planning, they are describing the plan to the players. The primary job of all Presidents, Project Managers, Engineers, and Military Officers is planning. We've all heard the following statement, "Let's go back to the drawing board." That's because life itself is dynamic and no plan is ever final.

How does any of this relate to you and your future? It's simply a suggestion that you need a plan for a better future. What lies ahead for you? A plan designed for you and by you, will give you something to look forward to. You will be in a state of joyful anticipation because you're getting a glimpse of your desirable future. This plan will point the way and give you the steps to follow. If you already have a plan be aware that plans can become stale and lose their power to inspire. Plans need to be refreshed because no matter how good your plan is, it will need to be brushed up along the way. Revisions are nothing to be discouraged about; all good plans are constantly under review so that the outcome can be perfected. When you revise or refresh your plan, you will become enthused all over again. Simply stated, a plan will keep you on-course toward your chosen destiny. You will have some good luck, but you can also expect some bad luck. Don't be discouraged, this would happen even if you chose to wander aimlessly.

Following a plan may seem like a drag to some, but for those who believe in their plan it is an exciting preview of coming attractions. A well-executed plan can turn what you imagined into a real-life experience. Anytime someone is thinking and planning their future, opportunities and rewards are more likely to appear, because the mind is primed to detect them. Planning also gives you a sharpened awareness of hazards. The minute you engage in planning you recall past mistakes. Emotionally, you relive the pain so you will avoid it in the future. Without a plan people have a tendency to forget past mishaps. This opens the door to a painful repeat. A plan helps, but it does not prevent accidents. The planner should be prepared to treat setbacks as opportunities to make corrections for a safer path forward.

When you're planning you are also creating belief and belief gives you the energy to get started, because action is the ultimate necessity needed to execute the plan. Look around everything you see cars, houses, bridges, even the fire-hydrant, they all started with a plan.

When your plan is laid out on paper, in your mind's eye, you will clearly see a vision of what your about to create. Don't get too excited, the most important thing to remember is that plans only pop into reality when they are put into action.

Chapter 25
Goal Setting

"A winner is someone who recognizes his God-given talents, works his tail off to develop them into skills, and uses these skills to accomplish his goals."

Larry Bird

Sugar Ray Leonard the great Champion boxer and Olympic gold medal winner gave us a real-life example of goal setting. He described what he did to succeed. He would focus for hours every day isolating, practicing, and perfecting just one single punch. In training he would work exclusively on a jab, hook, or other punch until he was satisfied that it was close to perfect. This champion even practiced things like running backwards for long periods; knowing you need to have defensive as well as offensive techniques in the ring. When he combined these finely honed skills, fight fans observed a master executing a magnificent performance. His boxing record in the ring will stand as a testament to his pursuit of excellence.

This same goal setting strategy can be applied any time a person wants to master a new skill or learn a new subject. Every expertise or performance can be broken down into basic building blocks. To become competent at swimming, typing, math, piano, or a new language you must complete a series of steps. When you start out to do something you've never done before, you have to start small. It is interesting to note, to reach success in any field the first step is most important. Without committing to take that first crucial step; you have no chance to become accomplished. It's simple logic that getting started is the most important act needed to attain any skill. A person who is serious about acquiring a new ability must have a daily time slot to practice and study their chosen pursuit. Without these key pledges, getting started and setting aside time, one would be choosing failure right from the start. To avoid such a self-imposed catastrophe, a person needs to make a firm decision to do whatever it takes.

A firm decision will determine your destiny. Once in motion a person must maintain an unrelenting will to win. How can you tell if you have what it takes? Listen to the words of Mark Spitz, who won 7 gold medals in the 1972 Olympics. "We all love to win, but how many people love to train?" you know the answer to Mark's question. Everyone understands that it requires discipline to train for a rewarding future. There is no other way. Without a daily program it's impossible to make constant progress. The commitment to daily practice must be high priority in your life; that's what separates the winners from the losers. If you need motivation imagine that your competitor is out there getting ahead of you.

Every subject you might wish to master can be broken down into small individual parts or acts. Start with baby steps, if you want to learn algebra you may have to go back and brush up on basic math. Keep on keeping on and until you feel some satisfaction from your efforts. If you're not making steady progress, you might try a target practice technique; move a little closer to the bull-seye, when it becomes too easy move further back.

The underpinning of every ability is repetition, as mentioned in an earlier chapter. Repetition is the mother of learning, skill, and habit, and achieving habit is the gold standard that locks in success. One little win leads to another little win as you gravitate towards excellence. Once your practice is working, you'll feel certain that you can become good at this. Overtime little repetitive acts mount up and soon you have prodigious ability. Once the new talent is yours, you can move on with even greater confidence and add a totally different skill to your repertoire. This type of goal setting can keep you happily involved in growing for the rest of your life.

Chapter 26
Getting Started

"If you have a dream, you can spend a lifetime studying, planning, and getting ready for it. What you should be doing is getting started."

Drew Houston

Everyone reading this book will have their own idea about what success should look like. It's likely my readers are kindred spirits who want to find ideas and techniques that will help them achieve their dreams of success. Deep inside, you know if you can bring to life what you want, it will bring you joy. The fact you are reading this book means you are looking for answers. You want to find better techniques so you can speed up your progress. There are lots of pillars upon which achievement is built. As a student of success, you'll likely agree with this partial list of traits needed to make progress. Focus, Desire, Discipline, Determination, Priority, Planning, Persistence. It's more than intimidating to know that these attributes are needed to achieve success. Don't feel overwhelmed because I left out the most important one that can bring all of these qualities into play naturally. It's the single ingredient you can't leave out if you are really serious about success. In fact, if you have this lone priority constantly in play, success is the most likely outcome. Getting Started! It is just that simple. Not just once, but over and over again you must get started. Is it hard to do? Yes, that is why many talented people who should have been big successes just couldn't pull it off. It's difficult, but on the plus side once you get yourself going, "It's as easy as taking candy from a baby."

We all know in any occupation every workday is a new start, I'm confident that you have great ideas and visions for a fabulous life. Here's how you can make it happen. Begin again and again, and things will fall into place. Not easy, but if your goals are worth it, get moving. Imagine how much sooner you can enjoy what you've dreamed about if you start now?

People often doubt that they have the drive or ability to get what they want, when truthfully all they need is immediate action. Don't let fear of mistakes stop you. You will make mistakes, everyone who seeks to accomplish something blunders along the way. Study the missteps, it's the best education you will every receive, because it helps you avoid mistakes going forward. Begin and like magic you'll find that you know what to do. Once you're immersed in activity, both opportunities and obstacles will arise. You take advantage of opportunities, and you will find ways to remove obstacles. You know what happens next, you enjoy the rewards activity brings you. Give yourself one little push forward, it can be the extra boost that put's you over the top. If you were to drive a car cross country you would need to start the car again and again because you would need to stop to eat and sleep, but you would likely reach your destination. The title of this book Unrelenting Little Efforts is you're your key to the good life. You know what you want, action is the way to get it. Action is your true friend, because you can't depend on luck or anyone else for your success. In fact, you can attract more support from others when they see you as a doer, the type of person they would like to be associated with. It takes just a little burst of will power to get moving and become a winner. You're reading this book which tells me you've got the desire to chase your dreams. Get started, just keep moving, just keep busy, just keep doing, and you'll be amazed at what you can accomplish.

Chapter 27
Starting Over

"When you're at the end of your rope, all you have to do is make one foot move out in front of the other. Just take the next step. That's all there is to it."

Samuel Fuller

While working with young trainees I discovered that no matter how motivated, intelligent, or talented they might be; at times they would get discouraged. Often, that discouragement shut down the good progress they were making. They did not realize that all they needed was a new start, and a slightly different approach to what they were doing. They would reveal to me that complications were causing them to lose confidence. I would tell them to try a new approach, and give them a little encouragement, and soon they were back on track. As interns in the field of Information Technology this was an opportunity for them to carve out a good career in a growing field. They were required to finish the tasks assigned to gain the competence they would need to become IT specialists. Persistence would almost guarantee a future opportunity, but it's hard to go on when you're discouraged. Some saw persistence as banging your head against the wall in useless frustration. In fact, persistence is simply starting over in a more ingenious way. This is best described in the words of F. Scott Fitzgerald: "*Vitality shows in not only the ability to persist but the ability to start over.*" I think that quote makes the point strong, there is great power in starting over. Quitting is also a great power because it brings everything to a halt, but it results in missed opportunities and unhappy feelings. Starting over is mandatory for achieving whatever you desire, nothing of consequence can be attained with zero problems. No matter how brilliant a person is; they will meet failure from time to time, and only by starting over can they turn failure into success. Each new start is a chance to approach the task at hand from a more practical viewpoint. That viewpoint comes from the lessons learned from each failed attempt.

Working with young people, I realized that we all have a champion within. A restart can bring the champion to the forefront. Once I persuaded these young people to believe in themselves, everything would change. What was once impossible for them; would now seem to be easily within their reach. Lethargy and apathy were replaced with the fire of determination.

We are most alive when we are making progress toward what we are seeking. We are on fire with high expectations, which gives us energy to complete the task we began. We cannot escape temporary failure, but with a little effort failure can be turned into success, by starting over. Baseball hall of fame pitcher Bob Feller, said this: "*Every day is a new opportunity. You can build on yesterday's success and put its failures behind and start over again. That's the way life is, with a new game every day, and that's the way baseball is.*"

Discouragement will push you in the direction of quitting and that awful feeling of defeat. Disruptions can and will occur, but you always have the power to make a fresh new start. Almost immediately upon such a decision, you will feel alive anticipating a brighter day. Adopt this starting over attitude and you'll always be on course to live the best life you've imagined.

If you feel anger don't quit, you can use that anger to push you through fear and reluctance. A new beginning is the key to getting what you want, so don't delay, restart your engine now. When you're discouraged you can choose to dawdle in anger and frustration, or you can start over. Often, you must choose between quitting and trying a fresh new start. Choose to start over and over again and you'll quickly complete the thing you started out to do and you'll feel great when it's done. That's the way you do it. Time is running out; don't delay, get started now. Start over and you're destined for success, all the setbacks will make your ultimate triumph that much sweeter.

Chapter 28
Recipe For Success

"The thing always happens that you really believe in; and the belief in a thing makes it happen."

Frank Lloyd Wright

A giant in the world of psychology William James, whose ideas have influenced the world, had this to say about belief: *"Believe that life is worth living and your belief will help create the fact."*

The Belief Recipe: This is a recipe for success, and you have all the ingredients on hand: Take a single desire, something you urgently hunger for. Then whip up a plan. Add a dash of determination to get started. Continuously pour in generous amounts of action; don't skimp on the action. Mix it all together until you have resolute persistence. Put it all in the hot oven of struggle. Next set the temperature to high by believing that you will get it. Allow the necessary time and voila you're now taking pleasure in the thing you desired. Save this recipe and feed these instructions to your mind when you want something. When your mind is in a state of belief it is obedient, and it will do your bidding, it always has, and it always will. The thing that makes this simple recipe foolproof is belief. Singularity of purpose backed with strong belief always gets results. First, believe in yourself. Next believe in your dream. Believe in the awesome power of getting started. Perish the thought of quitting. True belief will lead to action. Now I will mix metaphors to make the point about belief stronger. Enthusiastic action is the vehicle that will take you all the way to accomplishment and the wonderful world you dream of. Speaking of vehicles; make strong note of the words from the man who put us all in the driver's seat. *"If you think you can do a thing or think you can't do a thing, you're right."* Henry Ford

Belief will also put you in the driver's seat on the road to success. Keep Henry Ford's words fresh in your mind as you drive towards your chosen destination. Check your belief often, if your belief is going down, you'll stall out. If you're full of belief, you are unstoppable, it's certain your dreams will be realized.

Chapter 29
Self-Belief

"Man is made by his belief. As he believes, so he is."

Johann Wolfgang von Goethe

Imagine if there were a miraculous way you could meet any challenge and pursue any desire with supreme confidence. There is such a powerful influence that is not only astonishing, but when you have it you are almost invincible. I'm talking about self-belief. *"A belief is not merely an idea the mind possesses: it is an idea that possesses the mind."* Robert Oxton Bolton

What you believe about you shapes and defines your life. Everyone has self-belief in some area of their life. If you believe you're a good dancer you will be inclined to dance when an opportunity appears. Believe the opposite and you will likely be a wallflower. When you see yourself as having good mechanical skills, you won't hesitate to fix things. If you believe you can sing you'll jump at the chance to do so. Do you see yourself as a funny person? If so you'll make an effort to be funny. One reason for your belief is that other people told you were funny, and that started a foundation for your belief.
In every area of life, you have an opinion about your innate ability. Obviously, it's helpful to think well of yourself because it allows you to be confident in nu-

merous situations. People assume they were born with whatever talent they have, but that's rarely true except for physical advantage, for instance basketball players being tall.

Everyone with 5 senses intact can learn almost anything. Look at young people and notice how proficient they are in the use of their smart phones. It would be preposterous to believe that they were all born with this talent and skill. Most people learn how to drive, yet no one views the crowded highways as proof that everyone is gifted with a natural ability to drive.

A person's abilities are formed by taking the repetitive action needed to develop skill. Your skills are the result of your desires, interests, likes, and dislikes. There has to be a catalyst and a resolve to bring any skill into reality. Look back to the beginning before you could drive, swim, type, or ride a bike, etc. You will find that your desire led to a belief in yourself that you could do it. Perhaps someone complemented you and that spurred you on. Belief that something can be done leads to the actual achievement. You would not endure the discipline needed to obtain a new skill unless you had self-belief.

Continued pursuit of a dream is inextricably linked to the conviction you will succeed. When self-belief, desire and repetition are linked, the odds for success are incredibly high. The stronger your self-belief the more often you find a way to win. Everyone falls short in some area of skill and achievement. Knowing this takes the pressure off when we fail in one of our pursuits. The old cliché "If at first you don't succeed try, try, again" might bring the success you're looking for next time. If you stopped short of gaining a skill, stop thinking that you don't have natural ability. Natural ability is overrated and possibly non-existent. Would Mozart have been a great musician if he had been born in the primitive jungle?

Giving up occurs when your self-belief is weak or absent, you lose all desire to continue. Positive or negative self-belief is the force that drives you on or stops you cold. Success is the result of progress that survives the inevitable setbacks. Genuine self-belief could be described as an unrelenting will to win. Failure occurs when your belief flips over into disbelief, and you stop trying.

Learning is the key to almost every benefit we gain in life. Sometimes a teacher, mentor, or trusted friend can help a person elevate their self-belief. They can teach, instruct, or simply give a person encouragement. Once this person gains some confidence their self-belief grows. This newfound belief helps them overcome reluctance and they make an attempt. Once self-belief is established it's like magic, people start doing things with ease they once thought impossible. To the neophyte they are amazed at their new power, but the ability to succeed was always there.

What are you good at? I know you are skillful at reading, and you enjoy using this skill that you developed in grade school. If you were illiterate and you didn't know how to read it might be difficult to convince you that you could make sense of all these little characters on this page.

When you attempt anything new, and you have a bad experience that can stop you cold. A person enters sales, and right away they experience rejection. The rejection is so painful they quickly decide sales is not for them. That experience makes them believe they are not cut out for sales. On the other hand, what happens if a person gets lucky on their first attempt at selling. They make a sale right away and it seems like easy money. That person is more likely to stick with sales because the initial reward led them to believe in future rewards. Eventually they will feel the sting of rejection, but the first win gives them enough confidence to go on believing that it's possible to win again. Many high school quarterbacks start out with a vision of becoming a superstar. That vision quickly fades if they are sacked often, feeling only pain and embarrassment. A good defensive line and a few touchdown passes might have created a high school hero with a promising future in football. Superstars have had enough winning experience to develop an extraordinary amount of self-belief. Do you think that Tom Brady has enough self-belief? Once a belief has been established it will usually be reinforced over time. An avid golfer has the belief they are good, and when they have a bad day they simply shrug it off as an anomaly. At this stage in his career Tiger Woods is struggling, yet he could easily defeat non-professional golfers. His self-belief has been reinforced by his total wins and world recognition that he is a champion golfer. People have a strong tendency to believe what you believe about yourself. Marilyn Monroe and a friend were walking back from a shopping trip through a street filled with shoppers. The girl walking along-side Marilyn was amazed that no one recognized the famous movie star out in public. When she asked her famous friend about this, Marilyn told her something to this effect: "That's because I'm Norma Jean. Do you want to see what happens when I'm Marilyn Monroe?" Then Marilyn assumed her movie star persona; instantly they were mobbed by autograph seekers. Everyone has a belief about themselves, and it creates the image they project to the world.

People transmit to others what they're feeling at the moment, joy, fear, anger, or irritation. We are always sending out subtle, subliminal signals. If someone smiles at you, and you have an image of yourself as a friendly person, you're likely to smile back. Your self-belief not only decides your actions, but it influences all aspects of your life, including your relationship with others.

All of us have far more potential than we are aware of. Our true capabilities are slumbering under a blanket of self-doubt. We're not born with positive or negative beliefs; we learn and adopt our beliefs. Convince yourself that something is possible, and such a belief will make it possible. Just imagine how your life will improve if you cast out self-doubt and replace it with can-do, self-belief. Adopt this outlook and you will see that your goals are within reach. Now, there is no doubt that you will live your dream life.

Chapter 30
Money and Wealth

"The lack of money is the root of all evil"

Mark Twain

The cover of this book symbolizes money and wealth. Few things are more honorable than the honest acquisition and use of money. Money provides food, shelter, education, health care, transportation, vacations, and warmth in the cold of winter. It provides all things necessary for existence and more abundant living. Through the ages many things have been invented that make life better for all of us. These improvements include language, music, cooking, medicine, tools, it's an endless list, but of all these advances money may be man's greatest invention! That may sound like blasphemy but follow along and see if you don't agree.

Money is simply a way for humans to serve other humans. We humans are as dependent on one another as bumble bees are in their society. We literally cannot exist without one another. Money provides an easy way for us to interact and exchange goods and services we want and need. Money simplifies the way we can serve each other. In ancient times before money was used; the barter system provided the same cooperative give-and-take between people. A fisherman could swap some fish for nuts, berries, and perhaps a chicken. Currency is nothing more than a convenient way to replace the cumbersome barter system. Without cash, credit cards, and mobile payments it would be impossible to have all the conveniences we have.

As an individual living in a wealthy country, you have millions of people serving you. Can you imagine having to make the clothes you wear or grow the food you eat? Perhaps you could, but it's almost certain that you enjoy the freedom of being able to buy those necessities. It would be impossible for individuals to build their car, computer, or smart phone. It's not something people reflect on, but we are totally dependent on the services of others from the moment we're born. In one sense, we human beings are compelled to serve each other to insure our own existence. If you think about it, it's remarkable that you have so many people competing to serve you. Yes, they're doing it for the money, but why should money have such a bad reputation when it feeds and clothes all of us. The competition between one another provides the very best at the least expense. The exchange of money advances the living standards of everyone. Money is our reward for service to others. If we look for the best thing that money can buy, it may be a peaceful world. Money is good for human relations; it requires cooperation between the service provider and the service receiver. This exchange of services causes dependency on those services. Now nations have to consider losing vital access to essentials if war breaks out. Nations are less likely to go to war when they depend on one another for important products like food, fuel, or technology. Just observe all the peaceful nations, who in the past, waged bloody warfare against one another. For centuries, horrific war raged on between many European nations. War was considered the norm, it was inevitable. These nations spoke different languages and had different customs. All that bloodshed ended less than one hundred years ago. Europeans now cross each other's borders to earn a little money, find a bargain, or relax on vacation. Across Europe everyone plays the role of merchant or buyer. Today war between European nations is unthinkable. As simplistic as it might sound, the exchange of money has helped maintain peace and prosperity. When mutual dependency exists, people have far less desire to destroy their provider or customer. The U.S.A. participated in World Wars I & II. We've made peace and now we're linked financially to many of our prior enemies. Both sides are benefiting from buying and selling each other's goods. Enemies who wanted to destroy each other are now striving to become the top providers of cars, TV's and other products to their former adversaries. Instead of pointing weapons of war, the peaceful nations are now promoting tourism. What people won't do for money. They now openly invite the violent enemies of the past to vacation in what was formally a war-torn land. Just imagine if this trend continues all nations will have a mutual dependency on one another. Then we can replace blood in the streets with money in the streets, and finally have peace on earth.

Chapter 31
Creativity

"You must not for one instant give up the effort to build new lives for yourselves. Creativity means to push open the heavy, groaning doorway to life."

Dalsaku Ikeda

Through creativity we can improve all aspects of our existence making life more pleasant and rewarding. Studies indicate most people underestimate the vast power of their own creativity. Creativity distinguishes humans from all other living species. We're the only creatures on earth that create things and solve problems to make life easier. Animals survive on instinct alone, but from earliest times our ancestors invented tools, weapons, and of course the wheel.

What exactly is creativity? It is simply bringing something into reality that first existed only as a picture in the mind. It could be anything, a game, song, or barbeque pit. If you were challenged, I have no doubt you could write a poem, learn to knit a sweater, or build a doghouse. Think back to when you were a child and remember some of your creative pursuits. Did you ever build a Lego skyscraper, a go-cart, or some other contraption? Even drawing a simple picture from imagination requires creativity. Creativity is your innate power, and activating it can change your life into what you desire it to be.

Be assured that you can tap into your creative power at will? A very simple technique for arousing your creativity, requires just a pen and pad of paper. Be willing to experiment and like most people you will discover that you are a very creative person, it's your nature. Here's how you can summon this power anytime you desire. Grab a pad of paper and make a list of all the ideas you have about some want, need, or subject important to you. The act of listing will cause you to go deep into thought, and related ideas will start to flow. Each idea tends to bring forth more ideas and new ideas seem to come out of the blue. This is your creativity at work. With this form of concentrated thinking, you'll uncover golden possibilities that never would have occurred to you in your daily routine. It's like digging for gold, you keep digging until you find a few nuggets. Putting your ideas on paper will stimulate your natural creativity. Experience this for yourself by writing down whatever comes to mind, it should be an idea that excites you.

Before you start writing expect the best. Positive expectancy preps your mind for optimum creativity. List something that you really want to make happen and imagine how it's accomplishment will improve your life and make you happy. This should be a pleasurable experience as you list the ideas you want to focus on. Keep in mind that active creativity can be life enhancing as it leads you into tackling projects you enjoy. Also, you'll begin to notice that practicing creativity enhances your ability to solve problems. This simple activity of listing your wishes on paper will lead to ideas that will improve your life, work, and home.

Repetition of this mental exercise could possibly become a life-long habit, resulting in more successful living. While you're focusing on things that enthuse you, you'll uncover this side benefit. Your inspired ideas will cause you to feel a burst of energy and a desire to follow up with action. This is the most important aspect of creativity, because without action nothing happens. What you clearly desire will evolve into reality once you combine creativity and action. Start using your natural creativity and what you imagine, and desire will be yours.

Chapter 32
The Incredible Average Person

Most of the well-known American success stories were started by average people of modest means, and all started relatively small.

A man named Jeff Bezos, started so small, he couldn't afford a much-needed fork-lift when he began his on-line bookstore, which we now call Amazon, by the way, Jeff is now the richest man in the world. An ordinary guy named Sam Walton opened a little five and dime store in a small town in Arkansas. His big idea was that the business would thrive if he could lower his already thin profit margins, perhaps you know the company he started, Walmart. Billionaire, Oprah Winfrey grew up as a poor kid in Mississippi. Clothing mogul Ralph Lauren started out as a clerk in a clothing store. W. Clement Stone was selling newspapers at 5 years of age to help support his widowed mother, he then went on to become an insurance salesman. He didn't stop until he built AON one of the largest insurance and finance companies in the world. The man who started Starbucks, Howard Schultz grew up in a housing complex for the poor, now he's a billionaire.

Let me tell you one more story of an incredible average person. Her name is Sara Blakely, she successfully found a way to help women solve a problem she solved for herself. Sara was a young woman who had worked as a Disney greeter and door to door salesperson. Her rags to riches story started when she had a little problem. She wanted to wear pantyhose under some jeans, but she didn't like the look of hose covering her feet. Simple solution: she cut the feet off her pantyhose. She liked the resulting look, because the pantyhose was not visible, but it still provided some shaping quality that she liked.

Inspired at her creation, she took the idea a little further. Experimenting, she came up with an idea to go beyond pantyhose to combine women's clothing with a built-in undergarment shaping material. She created a clothing line that has helped women look shapelier, the company is called Spanx. People in sales and marketing would never describe it in the following way, but what she did was to reinvent and bring back the girdle. Most people would agree that creating such a product and bringing it to market was brilliant, and to think she's just an average person. You might suspect that she had to have some background in the clothing business. In her own words: "I'd never worked in fashion or retail. I just needed an undergarment that didn't exist."-Sara Blakely. So, you might ask: Did Sara make millions from her idea? Not exactly, Sara, at the time, became the youngest female billionaire in history.

I could keep adding people to this list until I had a book large enough to make the Guinness Book of World Records, but the average person would never have time to read it. I just thought there may be some incredible average people reading this and I just wanted to inspire them.

Chapter 33
Imagination

"Imagination is the beginning of creation. You imagine what you desire, you will what you imagine, and, at last, you create what you will."

George Bernard Shaw

Imagination can enhance both your inner and outer world. Our personal world is in a constant state of change; that is because life itself is dynamic. In time our outer world becomes a mirror image of our inner world. What you imagine is the human driving force that gives our mind consciousness. It is in a constant state of mental vibration; the closest thing to a perpetual motion machine that one can think of. Imagination is the starting point for our actions. In this chapter we'll discuss how imagination can work for us or against us. We'll discover how to replace impotent imagination with unlimited imagination.

A Limitless Resource

"Every man builds his world in his own image. He has the power to choose, but no power to escape the necessity of choice."
Ayn Rand

If you've read this far, you likely are searching for something that will dramatically change your life and your world for the better. It's obvious that you have a degree of determination, and that's the big imperative one needs for spectacular achievement. Many people start self-help books, but few finish and fewer act upon what they've learned. You've come this far so you have a thirst for knowledge. I want you to be rewarded for your loyalty in staying with me. You deserve to learn of the magic that glues all of this together. I have been promising you a crucial answer. You will not be disappointed if you can grasp and implement what I am about to relate to you. Act on this idea, and it will bring you success and happiness, while elevating your life to where you want it to be. It's a big promise I know. Yet it's one of the least difficult things you'll ever have to do. This should be relatively easy because you're already doing it. Sometimes you do it right, and you go up, and sometimes you do it wrong, and you go down. This is the ultimate human driving force. It's your imagination and we are going to explore this limitless resource.

Climbing to the Top

In order to use the power of your imagination correctly you will need to climb four mountains. The four mountains only exist in your imagination. Yet anytime you are contemplating an ambitious project, the four mountains are facing you. In fact, you may never start your adventure, because the mountains appear too steep and intimidating for you to climb. By the way, if these mountains weren't in your way you would already be enjoying the marvelous thing that you envision.

What are the Four Mountains?

Mount Impossible

The biggest mountain you face is Mount Impossible. The belief that something is impossible is a mountain too difficult for anyone to climb. You just look up at it, and you're powerless. The conviction that something is impossible violates the first secret of success. "The First Secret of Success is the Belief that it Can Be Done, and You Can Do It."

This imaginary mountain is truly the most challenging. Even when you don't see this mountain; people around you will point it out. In fact, you can seek out the advice of experts and they will describe this mountain in scary detail. Don't even try to climb this mountain-you can't! If you're going to accomplish something significant in your life; you are going to have to mentally demolish Mount Impossible down to the ground, and then climb the other three. Once you have decided that something is impossible; take note because it might not be too long before you see someone else doing it.

Mount Time

The next imaginary mountain you will have to climb is Mount Time. If you have imagined that you have no time, you have convinced yourself that you can't have whatever you've been dreaming about. You may be living in a dream world called some-day. Don't be fooled; 'some-day' is actually an imaginary prison, located in a dungeon in this mountain. As long as it exists in your imagination there is no escape. Yes we're only imagining all of these things. We're imagining because: We have to imagine success in order to move towards success. We have to imagine failure in order to move in that direction. Without a dedicated slice of time nothing will happen no matter how vividly you've imagined the future you seek. Without climbing Mount Time you can't get to the next two mountains, and that means you will die unfulfilled at the foot of this mountain.

Fortunately the same imagination that created the dungeon prison Some-Day in Mount Time, can also help you escape the prison and climb the towering majesty of Mount Time. Obviously what you've set your sights on is something so important to you that I assume you are willing to give it highest priority. Imagine, just for a moment, how wonderful it would be if you make time by finding some less important thing in your life to eliminate. Imagination lets you gain entry to the guarded places of sacred time in your mind that are marked-Do Not Enter!!! Imagination lets you bypass the guarded places in our mind and enter these sanctuaries. As we roam through our mental caverns; let's take a chance and enter the hollow where our permanent daily priorities lay fixed. This exploration can be fun, and just imagine if we can discover something way down at the bottom of this mind cavern which contains our daily priorities. We just might be able to find something of little importance that's using up precious time. There see; we've found some predictable daily doings that have been here so long they're dust covered. Looking at them we can see that some of these acts are no longer useful in our life. This is a great discovery; because once we throw them out, we have the time needed for our new adventure. Like magic your imagination has found all the time you need to climb Mount Time. This newly found time must be sacrosanct, a fixed priority in your life. Now you will need to take charge and stomp out all the nonessential things that are cluttering up your day. While we're trying to find time: Is it possible that there some things you do that cause you to dilly dally? Perhaps you can zip right through these things with no real loss. Can you do a little less of some daily practice? I'm not saying eliminate, you just want to streamline your routines. I believe a winner does a little rather than nothing at all. Setting aside a specific time slot is the proverbial first step to success. One more thing to remember as we get set to climb Mount Time: A most worthy goal is to always be on the alert for ways to save time.

Mount Obstacle

Once you're on top of Mount Time your next challenge is conquering the mountain we called Mount Obstacle. This mountain is a little tricky because the obstacles keep changing step by step as you climb up this mountain. You don't want to fall down this mountain and get killed. So you must take safety precautions. At all times you must clearly identify the obstacles before you, and go over, under, around, or through them. Since everyday on this mountain can bring new obstacles you must constantly identify the ones holding you back. In between conquering the obstacles; a good question to ask your-self is: What am I doing now that is working to move me onward and upward? Knowing what's holding you back and being aware of what's moving you forward, is knowledge that can speed you to the top.

Now you've obliterated Mount Impossible, and you've stood at the top of Mount Time and Mount Obstacle; consider yourself a full-fledged victorious climber. It's obvious you have a good imagination. You can take solace in the fact that you have more drive than most. You've met three big challenges and you've proved to be a worthy conqueror. Now the question is, can you skew up enough courage to tackle the last mountain that kills almost every climber - Mount Fear.

Mount Fear

You say you've come too far to be stopped by Mount fear. Very well; you will need to be aware of the hazards. This mountain becomes foggy; so the vision of where you're going becomes blurred out in the fog of doubt. The fog can become so thick that doubt turns into fear. This mountain is cluttered with the bones of strong people who were vanquished by fear. As you go up this mountain, your mind will swing like a pendulum, from confidence to doubt and back again Doubt is the one thing that can bring your dream-quest to a sudden halt and send you sliding down the mountain. Doubt can pile up, turn into fear, and right before your eyes; you've recreated Mount Impossible out of a frightful illusion. The truth is, it is hard to persist when you are in the fog of doubt, especially when doubt turns to fear. Persist you must. Keep going through the fog of doubt and fear. Fear is worse than doubt, if fear sets in it will cause you to freeze up in the fetal position right here on the side of Mount Fear. Tell me please that you don't want to be one of those poor souls whose dreams have died on Mount Fear. Just keep moving forward, have the courage to take just one more step. Soon the fog of doubt and fear will lift, and the sunshine of confidence will reappear. But don't be deceived, the fog of doubt will return again and again before you reach the top. You can count on it. Don't stop; keep going fear is mostly an illusion. Thankfully you have persistence, and it will take you right to the top through the dense fog. Your determination means you've decided to live, so you pushed beyond doubt and fear. You're moving up to the wonderful world of big success. Now you can see the top, and you realize you're about to conquer Mount Fear. Now your glorious vision becomes bright and clear and there's no stopping you. "An idea, is salvation by imagination." Frank Lloyd Wright

In your imagination you've conquered these four mountains and that kind of thinking can put you on top of the world. You've taken this imaginary journey up the mountains, and all it required was your vision. This mountain allegory is simply the big secret I've been alluding to. Your current reality began with your imagination. To this point in your life, you are the creation of your own fantasies, and so am I. We have become the result of the cumulative effect of our imagination. I hope that this journey has convinced you that you can imagine your future. So why not choose the brightest future you can envision?

Chapter 34
Habit

"Achieve success in any area of life by identifying the optimum strategies and repeating them until they become habits"

Charles J. Givens

I've introduced the following sentence a number of times in this book because I believe it is the key to understanding how we have become who we are. "Repetition is the mother of learning, skill, and habit." Habit is the gold standard if it enhances the life we are living. Repetitive action over time inscribes biological circuitry in our brain which directs our activities without much conscious effort on our part. Most of our thoughts and actions have been relegated to habit, these repeated routines are so interwoven into our life that we don't even realize we're on autopilot most of the time. Established habits often have a start button, that is they are trigged by certain activities. Coffee in the morning starts the smoker smoking. Enter your car, get behind the wheel, automatically you perform what is needed to start driving. These are things we do without much forethought. A combination of both good and bad habits are influencing our choices and consequently controlling our life. A prevalence of good habits can ensure our success and make our lives more comfortable.

In a sense, a good habit is like a faithful servant always at your beck and call. A good example of this is driving. Driving is simply a set of skills you learned and molded into a habit. When you were learning to drive you said things to yourself such as: I need to turn on the ignition and while my foot is on the brake, I'll move the lever to drive, next I'll press the gas pedal etc. Now you do it without thinking, it's simply a good habit, your mind is free to think of other things. Good habits can turn our wishes and hopes into reality. We refer to the habits that perform like this as skills. Skills are habits that give us the expertise to do something that is usually involved or complicated. Like playing a musical instrument, repairing a car engine, building a bird house etc. All these complex abilities are made up of minor skills we've learned along the way. General Colin Powell describes it this way. *"If you are going to achieve excellence in big things, you develop the habit in little matters. Excellence is not an exception, it is a prevailing attitude."* To acquire intricate skills involves a persistent effort to gain competence, we are only willing to make the effort if we have a strong desire to achieve gratifying objectives. Our nemesis in this life are the bad habits we've acquired. Living successfully means we have a minimum of bad habits and a predominance of good habits. A bad habit delivers pleasure, but over time they cause disappointment, pain, and can even lead to premature death. Drinking to excess, smoking, or taking street drugs deliver instant pleasure and they can easily become habits that are hard to shake. It's common knowledge as to the long term affects they have. Destructive habits keep you in their control, they make you feel helpless, and of course this leads to unhappiness.

With this in mind let's turn our focus to developing good habits. The more duties and burdens you can turn over to your personal servant habit the easier your life will be. Good habits are invisible helpers who handle the mundane details of our daily life. You only have so much time and it is peppered with both good and bad habits. Successful living is simply a predominance of constructive behaviors. Imagine if you could amass so many good habits that it would fill your time and crowd out your bad habits? We know from experience that habits are the result of repetition, and the amount of repetition needed is uncertain, but likely dependent on the amount of pleasure generated by the activity. Once you establish a useful habit it becomes almost effortless for you to perform the action needed. Good habits are a comfortable way of functioning because they save you time and effort. You've heard the old saying "We're all creatures of habit." It's true, and I'm sure you've developed at least some of the following useful habits: Driving, exercising, shaving, grooming, typing, sending email, etc. Your good habits are working for you all the time. You don't think much about simple everyday activities like tying your shoes, brushing your teeth, or buckling your seat belt, you just do it. Once you master more complicated procedures like golfing, swimming, sailing etc. you forget how challenging it was before you became at ease with these activities. Now they're habits, and your reflexes are trained so that you can perform with confidence. If a desire for excellence prevails you will always be seeking to become even more competent. We know that developing good habits requires a strong desire and a firm commitment because it takes time, repetition, and dedication before a habit is fixed permanently in your unconscious mind.

Some skills are so important for living a worthwhile existence you would likely make an all-out effort to acquire them if somehow they were missing from your life. It is almost impossible for you to imagine how difficult life would be if you were illiterate. Learning to read and write would require a massive effort. As an adult, would you have the will to practice, drill, and rehearse to establish the habit of literacy? Without habits your life would be a constant struggle just to get through the routine of a normal day.

With some forethought you can choose to add new habits that will enhance your life. You can also improve current habits to make sure that you have the most productive practices possible. Just Imagine the possibilities. With these goal-seeking habits you will be able to achieve your life's objectives with the ease, comfort, and the speed that habit delivers.

Habit, Time and Place

The absolute essential requirement needed to form a good habit is a specific time and place where you will act out the necessary routine until the fledgling habit is firmly established. A good habit is simply a way to turn some goal-seeking activity over to your robotic unconscious. Once the habit is set; you can function with little effort. We never know how long it will take to establish a valuable habit, but two things we do know, it takes repetition, and it is worth the effort.

Forming good habits requires struggle in the beginning, but once established, habits do all the work. This is an important realization because actively or inactively we are creating daily routines that become habits. It makes sense for us to choose activities that will carry us forward to make life more pleasant. We all operate under the concept of cause and effect, and there is no escape from cause and effect. Life is cumulative, and you are either growing in positive ways or you are establishing negative routines. Over time the power of cumulative effect will work in your interest if positive activities are dominant in your life.

You know you must pay the price for all good things. The price is steep for acquiring a winner's habit. You will need to make a firm commitment, and you must assign a specific area where you will practice, and most important you need to set the exact daily start time. If you have what it takes to do all this, you will acquire the superb ability you are aiming for, it's just a matter of time. With this type of resolve you gain membership in the ranks of those who enjoy successful living.

Desire Is The Power Needed To Create Winning Habits

Can there be anything more exhilarating than being convinced you are about to live out one of your exciting dreams. Remember how important it was for you to learn how to ride a bike, drive, swim, dance, or play a musical instrument. That's the power of desire, you believe in your dream, and you act to make it real. Even if you cannot recall exactly how strong your desire was, you were enthused as you looked forward to the exciting endeavor. Since desire is the basis for the skills you now possess, why not continue to use this power which has worked so well for you in the past. What do you desire? It can be yours following the same formula you used successfully in the past. True desire is powerful, it can help you achieve all the wonders you can dream up. We don't think much about how we developed an ability; we just use it to our advantage.

Awareness of your current capabilities gives you confidence you can develop new skills. Every talent you acquire is sure to enhance your life now and continue to serve you in the future. Imagination is your highest power; it can generate the strong desire needed to attain winning habits. You envision what you want and imagine how good you will feel when it is yours. Desire wells up and intensifies. Inflamed desire is the driving force that gets you moving and keeps you going until your wishes turn into reality. Once you form the vision in your mind, it's done, you believe it's possible, and you act it out. Soon what you desired is yours, and you add one more power to your repertoire of talents.

Being Reward Minded Establishes Good Habits.

To purposefully establish a new habit, you must be reward minded, the expectation of enjoyment is vital. Unless there is some pleasure associated with an activity, it is unlikely the brain will lay down the circuitry that leads to the formation of a habit. The reason bad habits form so easily is they promise and deliver an immediate reward. The incentive you need to start with is the belief that the prized behavior you seek to develop is easily within reach. You want to feel certain that your efforts will lead to a happy outcome. The habit you desire to develop must be important to you because distractions are many and you can easily be lured away from your purpose. Often the thing we're distracted by is some trivial frivolity. If you're lured off course, the minor indulgence will leave you unsatisfied and wallowing in failure. The sad part of trivial cravings is that they never deliver the pleasure promised, they always disappoint. If a quest is important a person can stumble, but they will get back up and start all over. Of course, quitting is always an option, but the consequence is too often misery, and no one wants to live a life of failure.

With a little thinking and planning you can break any objective down into small doable steps. Now you simply follow the action plan you made for yourself. For example, you have a get together with friends in a week and you are a few pounds overweight. You decide to lose those extra pounds so you can look your best when you see them. You are smart so you write down simple things you will do to make sure you will lose the weight. Your list might include putting smaller portions of food on your plate, resisting snacks, drinking more water, exercising more, walking every day, etc. If the reward is rigidly fixed in your mind, and you believe it will work, you are likely to continue losing the weight. The reward: You are looking good when you meet your friends. This type of planning can work for any desired goal, and the key benefit occurs if this becomes a life-long habit to keep you at your ideal weight. By constantly focusing on the reward, you are much more likely to do what is needed to succeed. Apply this emphasis of being reward minded and your expectation of pleasure will keep you focused and motivated.

If you ardently desire an outcome, it becomes an obsession, and you are not only willing to do what needs to be done, but you feel compelled do it. Excited with anticipation you will chase the reward, day after day, week after week. Ultimately, you will be delighted when you gain the good habit you determined to develop, and your successful behavior is now your normal routine. You're happy because you are living successfully, it's the way you were meant to live.

Chapter 35
Something To Look Forward To

When most people are asked to reflect on the best time in their life, they have to stop and think. There were times for sure when their emotions took them to exhilarating heights, but most people are still waiting for that 'absolute best time in their life' which has yet to appear. We all know that hope springs eternal, and that is a blessing because high expectations make life more enjoyable here and now. You may have seen people on a quiz show, jumping for joy when the prize to be won is a trip to Hawaii, or a brand-new car. They may only win the consolation prize, but at least in that moment they were happy in anticipation. People have the same joyous experience when they plan an exotic vacation or when they decide to buy a dream house or car. Just thinking about it makes them happy.

If you are in sales or if you've ever taken a sales course there is a basic rule for success that you must learn. It's a brilliant tactic, but it's plain old common sense. The more benefits you can point out, the more likely you are to make the sale.

Together let's explore some of the benefits of looking forward. Anticipating simple pleasures like a walk in the park, having a good meal, or intending to watch a movie makes the current moment bright. Anything that promises fun can lift your spirits. This is a good thing because living in positive expectation helps us perform our daily duties in good spirits.

When you imagine something better down the road, that can change your whole future by motivating you to go after it. Everything starts by envisioning the future, that vision precedes getting married, starting a career, or beginning a hobby you find interesting. Expecting the best can turn you into a go-getter giving you that boost of energy that gets you started on your way to a win. You cannot help but feel good when you are certain that the reward that you planned and worked for is about to happen.

When you picture exciting coming attractions for your life, your whole world seems bright and jovial. The people around you are alert to this vibe, and they likely will pick up your cheery optimism. We know the opposite is true. When a person has a bad attitude, it can infect those around them. One person with a foul mood can dampen the spirits of everyone. Holding bright expectations will keep you from going down this dark road. We could go on and on filling this book with the benefits of being optimistic by looking to the future.

The most important advantage is that we are always moving in the direction of our dreams. You've always heard that you must hold fast to your dreams, let's explore the reason for this rule. When you have a vision of your place in the sun, and you are relentless in its pursuit, you will get to that future. Not tomorrow of course, but that's the direction you're moving in, and soon enough you'll arrive. Along the way you will need to refresh and possibly modify your dream to reach it.

If the thing you've imagined is totally impractical you can still make good and reach a reasonable replica of your glorious objective. You must be flexible, always learning, adjusting, and making the little changes needed to go forward. Be on the alert, your dream will fade unless you constantly dwell on it and refresh the picture of paradise you first imagined.

After seeing all these benefits, perhaps you'll adopt this idea of always having something to look forward to. Can you think of a simpler more pleasant way to improve your life? It's true you are only imagining possibilities, but possibilities often become realities. It's an exciting way to live, something good is always about to happen.

Chapter 36
Choose Belief Over Doubt

Can we really control our destiny? Imagine if someone could draw up a personalized life plan for you to become super successful. It would lay out all the detailed steps you need to follow for success. The plan would be as clear as an architect's blueprint allowing you to see in advance what the end result would be. It would be a fabulous vision describing a lifestyle you would be excited to embrace.

All you have to do is follow the simple step by step instructions, and voilà you arrive at a wonderful time and place. You now live in a magnificent home with the finest chefs creating fantastic meals for you. You are surrounded by loved ones and friends. A team of health experts train you to get fit and control your weight. Aladdin would be jealous of you, snap your fingers and people appear to serve you. Everyone is committed to making sure your way of life is superlative. Tutors and instructors help you master any sport or skill you desire. Simply follow the plan and you are living a fantastic life where fun, travel, entertainment, anything you desire is within reach. You feel so privileged you're compelled to set up a charitable institution to help the less fortunate everywhere.

At this point you may be thinking who could possibly believe this, it's all so improbable. This is not a fairy tale, it's no secret that there have been people who have lived like this throughout history. We're not just talking about kings and queens. I'm sure you can easily recognize some of the more recent names, Steve Jobs, Bill Gates, Jeff Bezos, Elon Musk, Warren Buffet, to name a few. What they have achieved seems beyond belief, but you know it's absolutely true. Your first thought might be these amazing people were all born with the proverbial silver spoon in their mouth. A quick check of their background will dispense with that assumption.

One thing you can be sure of, they all passionately believed in what they wanted, and acting on that belief produced their remarkable outcomes. These believers did what they wanted to do, and now everyone can see the results they foresaw. Is it possible to raise self-belief, as well as belief in one's dreams? The answer is yes. Everyone can raise their sunny beliefs up a notch, simply by lowering the heat from doubtful thoughts. It's a winning strategy to focus on belief, because as it grows, doubt will start to wither away and die.

How can we possibly start believing in a better future when it seems unlikely, and doubt is our strong suite? A dream can start as a little flicker of fire in your mind, now you're getting excited thinking about all the wonderful possibilities. Suddenly caution steps in and you think of all the hard work needed. Another reality check crosses your mind, it could all be for nothing. These thoughts will stomp out the most worthwhile dream, and all your left with is the smoke of disbelief. Our lives are a battle between doubt and belief; belief must win for you to succeed.

Isn't it true you either believe or you don't believe in something? What makes us sure that we can do certain things? Isn't it because we have done the thing before, or we have performed a similar act in the past? Sometimes we will see another person in action, golfing, cooking, dancing, and we can see ourselves doing the same thing. We think, it's not that difficult, and it looks like fun. In that moment a life changing event occurs, the formation of a belief. If we hold that newborn belief, we can try to do the thing we've envisioned. With just a hint of determination, we might add that ability to the repertoire of things we can do.

Remember when you were a child, people would ask you, what do you want to be when you grow up? It is easy for a child to believe all sorts of possibilities, they could be a singer, actor, teacher, fireman, etc. Limits were not something that crossed your mind when you were young. What is amazing is that we were all closer to the truth in those early days. Disappointments along the way have filled us with caution and doubt. We fear chasing after the opportunities that could improve our tomorrows. Now we're all grown up, we've become wiser, we've put limits on our once unlimited belief. It's so comforting to wrap ourselves in a security blanket. If we could get back some of that childlike courage, we might believe in ourselves again and do great things. It's never too late to make a commitment to believing, we can imitate those who followed their childish dreams and climbed the highest mountains.

Study the successful in any field and you will find they traveled through a blizzard of failures, but their belief kept them moving forward and they reached the sunshine of success. Winners are totally convinced of what they want, consequently they are driven to keep on going. They have to deal with failure of course, but they see all failures as stepping stones they must climb to reach their ultimate desire.

Once a person attempts any new activity, they feel a little uncomfortable or even clumsy. Often in the beginning a person will feel their new but fragile confidence starting to melt. They are on the thin ice of a newly formed belief. If they have the good sense to keep on trying, their belief will solidify, and they will make progress. No matter what a person chooses, the starting point will always involve a modicum of belief, which is needed to help erase any competing doubt and fear. Belief is the start button for any major undertaking in life. You must first convince yourself before you start a business, work on an invention, write a book, or begin a career. The bigger the dream the more convincing you'll need. Attempting a new interest such as tennis, guitar, sky diving, hang gliding, all will need your confident internal voice telling you, you can do that.

We're all stuck in the mud without belief, we need to be convinced that we can do the things we'd like to do. Of course, we also need to be assured that what we choose will be rewarding.

Developing belief is just the tip of the iceberg. To have constant deep below the surface belief, it must be perpetually nurtured and encouraged. Because life is dynamic and everchanging, your belief will constantly be challenged, wavering from conviction to uncertainty.

Fortunately, the fix is simple. When you are starting to lose confidence in yourself or your idea, you must stop this creeping doubt immediately. Grab whatever is available to write on and make a list of all the reasons for you to keep on believing. You'll be amazed, there are always more powerful reasons to believe than to disbelieve. Keep listing all you can think of until your courage is back. When you've completed your list, you'll find encouraging ideas continue to flow through your mind all day long.

You can determine your destiny if you keep believing in yourself and your dream. Belief keeps you moving towards your desired reality. Banish doubt, and you'll have no alternative but to find yourself living in the marvelous world you imagined.

Chapter 37
The Most Unlikely Helper

Where can we possibly find the time and energy for self-improvement in a world full of constant demands and distractions. Health concern is probably a high priority in your life, so you need to find the time to exercise. Of course, you want to maintain a certain amount of strength, speed, flexibility, and balance so your fitness program needs to address all these concerns. If you are like most people, you are also trying to lose or maintain weight.

Aside from health and fitness, you must do what is necessary to finance and maintain your living space. You need to make sure you have enough money for the necessities of life, medical expenses, and of course you need some entertainment, and a vacation every now and then. If you have kids, helping them is certainly on your agenda.

The demands of daily living never stop coming. When you're young you need to think about the fact that you are getting older and consequently the time will come when you want to be financially secure. All of this is enough to make a person tired and weary, how can anyone possibly keep up, never mind get ahead, in this rat race?

Well, I am going to introduce you to a helper I doubt you've ever considered to be a helper. When I first disclose your secret helper, you'll probably reject the idea. At first, you may see it as a form of human frailty, or an exasperation to be avoided. If you feel that it is an exasperation and also negative, I will totally agree with you, and this may actually be something you should not get involved with. You decide. I only bring it to your attention because it works. You may conclude that although your helper is negative, the help is worth it. Possibly if you accept this helper's power boost, it can get you moving to accomplish things you want to get done.

All progress comes from discontent, but it needs to be intense to move people to become productive. A couch potato can be miserable, and still not have the slightest intention to engage in active living. Discontent is always part of procrastination, yet people who put important things off, generally continue to do so. People who work hard all day doing their job have little energy or desire to do extra activities that would surely improve their circumstances.

I don't like being negative, but we have to do this to expose your not so nice helper. Do you remember the last time someone insulted you? What about the time you were unjustly punished in school, work, or embarrassed in front of family or friends? Can you still feel the pain? How about the time you were mortified when someone criticized you for something you did or didn't do. Do you remember the person who was no more capable than you, yet they acquired a better, house, car, and lifestyle? Remember the person who really hurt you, will you ever be able to forget? If you have never had an experience as just described, I can't help you, because you've led a charmed life, and you don't have a secret helper.

Just in case you think of something, I'll reveal your most unlikely helper now. The power lies in all the infuriating moments you endured in your life. These incidents are likely still burning hot whenever you recall them. Good old jealousy, anger, resentment, and outright hatred can get you aroused in a productive way. This powerful volcano within you always has your emotions on the verge of eruption, making you feel miserable, but if you direct this energy, it can be your secret helper. This energy can be harnessed, and it can motivate you to muscle your way to the top. You can push your way through the wall of fear, fatigue, and reluctance.

Is this truly a hidden reserve of energy? Yes, and it is more abundant than you can imagine. Remember the couch potato described above, a house fire would change everything. The lazy person would disappear, and a superhero would emerge. Running through the house, our newborn dynamo would warn everyone to get out, while placing a call to 911 for help. This is the same type of energy the secret helper provides.

It's a competitive world and with this newfound energy you can sprint ahead of the competition. Hopefully, the competition is unaware of the secret helper, otherwise this could be a real contest. Then again, the world has prospered greatly from competition, and we know there can be more than one winner. We are all competitive, deny this if you will, but you're not going to fool mother nature, she knows that deep down inside you are a competitor.

An important point must be made, revenge may be sweet, but it is also stupid, mother nature wants us to be smart and not spend energy striking back, which will not improve life one iota. Remember the old saying. "Living well is the best revenge."

Now that we've found this hidden secret helper who provides us with a store of energy, how do we tap into it, and what should we do with it? You can use the energy to do the things you've always wanted to do. You just imagine your rival having a better life than you, or your competitor becoming more fit, or thinner than you. Conjure up any infuriating happing that gets you riled up. This really works to get your competitive juices flowing. Your secret helper turns the ignition key and gets your engine started. Not revengeful action, but positive action that improves your life in some desirable way. Take enough constructive action to fix your life and your nemesis would be envious of your accomplishment. Action is the foundation for all progress and success, things only become possible when you are in action.

It's a strange phenomenon that occurs, your partner, children, friends, and everyone close, didn't lift a hand to help you. Yet out of nowhere, your old nemesis showed up to become your number one helper. It's wonderful, every time you face a distasteful or difficult task you call on this unpleasant outlier who's sure to help you. This most unlikely helper unfailingly delivers the infuriating powerful urge within you, to get even. You just decide to show this haunt from the past, that you are a champion, and you immediately start proving yourself. Once in action you realize that you are not only productive, but you also feel good. Once this becomes habitual, you will find that the one who haunted you, now helps you. With this help you are becoming the winner you always knew you could be.

Chapter 38
Calm, Cool, and Collected

A most admirable way to live, is to be calm, cool, and collected. When we feel in control of our life, we are at peace, things seem to be going our way. In a calm state of mind, we can think clearly and focus on what's important at the moment. What you do now can improve future moments and make your whole life a series of successes.

A person who is at ease when others are flustered, has the aura of a king or queen. Calmness and confidence go hand in hand. Often a person who is not seeking to be a leader arrives at that position by default. We naturally see calmness as a sign of strength, and we look up to a person who has unshakeable confidence. A quiet composure almost demands respect. When someone has this type of serene disposition, we sense leadership, and we're inclined to follow the lead of such a person. Listen to the words of famed football coach Tom Landry. "Leadership is a matter of having people look at you and gain confidence, seeing how you react. If you're in control, they're in control."

However, the most important form of leadership is leading one's-self. We must always be prepared to be in command of ourselves because adversity is always around the corner. Self-confidence is a byproduct of learning how to remain calm and tranquil when challenged by difficulties. Calmness is our natural state, but is easily disrupted, so maintaining it is more of an acquired skill. We can develop this ability when we purposefully remain calm, when meeting our daily challenges. Life is a magnificent experience, but daily living involves a never-ending stream of disruptions. Every person has survived numerous setbacks, but we all want to go on enjoying life as much as possible. Having the strength and courage to handle adversity is possible. Winning life's battles begins when you remain calm. Blowing off steam like a boiling tea kettle set's you up for a scalding loss. In a calm state you can control and direct your escalating energy and win. What are the thought patterns that can help us keep our composure? Being optimistic encourages us and calms us down because we're looking forward to better and brighter days. We can take solace in the fact that we're alive, and so far we've solved every problem we've faced, or at least we've learned to live with our current situation. Even if circumstances have left us with a dreadful condition, we can still love the life we're living, there's always something to be thankful for. In fact, being grateful is a wonderful attitude that can contribute to our serenity. Once a person has developed the habit of remaining calm life takes on a soothing glow as our confidence and spirits are tranquil. In this peaceful state all of life's wonders can be fully enjoyed. We only get one shot to savor this wonderful miracle we call life, it's most delightful if we can remain calm, cool, and collected.

Chapter 39
Resolutions

"Our daily decisions and habits have a huge impact upon both our levels of happiness and success."

Shawn Achor

Every January people make New Year's Resolutions, and a month later most people can't remember what the resolution was. Why do so many of these resolutions fail? Most people do not keep their resolutions, because they're not really resolutions, they are more like wishful thinking. These lukewarm promises do not vibrate in the heart and soul, and they quickly evaporate into thin air. They never had a chance of becoming real as they were crowded out by the mundane demands of everyday life. Too bad, because resolutions can make our life better, let's explore how.

Strong emotions, either positive or negative, are what keeps a resolution locked into the mind. Writing it down on paper is almost mandatory for a resolution to have a chance at survival. Listing all the reasons why you want, what you want, can intensify your resolve. These actions indicate that you are serious, and they will help give your resolution a solid foundation. Commitment is the most powerful way to lock your resolution in place. That requires you make a daily review of the resolution, where you can list additional reasons why you should persist. This is often referred to as keeping the dream alive.

Only when the promise to yourself is locked in emotionally will you have a resolution with a fighting chance of survival, and still you have one more hurdle to go over. You must set aside a sacred time and space for you to act on the resolution. You must do all of this otherwise you'll put the kibosh on your dream. Don't let that happen, follow through, you can do this. Go look in the mirror so you can identify the person who is responsible for making all this happen. Yes, you are the dream maker and it's your responsibility to follow through with action. Action is the ultimate power that transforms visions into reality. Stick with the resolution and it will deliver the reward you expect and with enough repetition it will become super easy to keep going because you'll turn the activity over to your faithful servant habit.

Chapter 40
Healthy, Wealthy and Wise

"Happiness is neither virtue nor pleasure nor this thing nor that but simply growth, We are happy when we are growing."

William Butler Yeats

It's true we are happiest when we journey towards reaching our full potential. Benjamin Franklin wrote the words *"Early to bed, early to rise, makes a man healthy, wealthy, and wise."* His words ring true if we are to grow successfully, we know it requires us to be actively striving during our waking hours. These words were written back in the 18th century and the world has changed a lot since then, but people have not changed. Franklin's message is still the gold standard to live by. Of course, rising early after a good night's rest sets the stage for doing what will make our life more fulfilling. When we have an objective that excites us, and we are making progress toward it, we are filled with joy. It does not matter our purpose, it could be a career, an investment plan, fitness objective, golf game, just fill in the blank. Working towards anything we truly desire elevates our spirits when we are convinced we'll soon have what we fervently want. The enthusiasm from expectation gives us the drive to make our success more likely. When you have a purpose like this you are living life to the full. This quote from Ben Stein describes this perfectly: "The human spirit needs to accomplish, to achieve, to triumph to be happy"

Anyone who would describe their life with the old saying, 'feeling down in the dumps' just needs to get into action by going after something that inspires them. As mentioned above the choices are limitless, anything a person desires to do, redecorating a room, learning to play tennis, writing a song, training to run a marathon, taking piano lessons, learning a new language, body building etc.

Of course, it takes courage for anyone to start a new project or activity because the elements of doubt and fear are always standing in their way. Since everyone deserves to live a happy life, doubt and fear must be crushed in order to pursue a worthy objective. The remedy for everyone stuck in neutral is to fearlessly get into action. I have used this quote from Mark Twain elsewhere, but people trapped in fear can do this and be free. "Do the thing you fear and the death of fear is certain." It's good advice because it gets you unstuck; now you feel the joy of living, doing something you've always wanted to do. It's a big reward, and it comes from just getting started. Now the challenge is to keep going.

Living in this world for any period of time, we know we can't avoid setbacks. Regardless of hinderances, we must be determined to push forward because giving up is too painful. No one has instant success, you can expect difficulties, but those who keep striving are soon rewarded with breakthroughs and progress. You must stick to something until you succeed, there is no other way. At some point you will enjoy victory and you will bask in the wonderful success you've earned. Ray Krock the man who brought Mc Donald's to your neighborhood endured tremendous difficulty before he achieved success. He had this little maxim by Calvin Coolidge posted above his desk. *"Press On - Nothing in this world can take the place of persistence. Talent will not: Nothing is more common than unsuccessful men with talent. Genius will not: Unrewarded genius is almost a proverb. Education will not: The world is full of educated derelicts. Persistence and determination alone are omnipotent."*

There are many benefits to self-development, and when we make progress in one area of our life it enhances our self-image and boosts our confidence. Now the power within is elevated and we raise our sights on even bigger and better attainments. Another benefit that comes from this successful lifestyle is the natural occurrence of a positive mood which influences our interactions with family, friends, and associates. When we are growing in an area we've chosen to work on, it increases our happiness, especially when we are gaining new skills. This personal development is extremely satisfying, and it can easily become habitual. Once habit is locked in, you'll carry your success with you wherever you go.

Chapter 41
How To Achieve Fame and Fortune

I thought, wouldn't it be nice if I could gather a large number of successful people and have each one tell us about their winning strategy. Then we could analyze each method and boil it all down to come up with an optimum strategy. Well, I found just such a group of people many of whom you already know due to their fame and fortune. The internet brought them all together for me.

This information is worth a fortune, and I do not want to chance getting something wrong. I want to get it to you as precisely as it was explained to me. For this reason, I've decided to stay in the background and let each one tell you their story directly. What I can tell you is they all seem to recognize the importance of goals and goal setting in their life.

Oprah Winfrey - Talk Show Host, Actress, and Business Woman said this: *"Energy is the essence of life. Every day you decide how you're going to use it by knowing what you want and what it takes to reach that goal, and by maintaining focus."*

Runner, Francie Larrieu Smith - Five time United States Olympic Team Member said: *"The most important factor for motivation is goal setting. You should always have a goal."*

Ted Turner - Billionaire founder of Cable News Network, had this piece of advice for people: "*You have to set goals beyond your reach so you always have something to live for.*"

Bo Jackson - The only Athlete to ever become an All-Star in both baseball and football told all his fans: "*Set your goals high, and don't stop till you get there.*"

Brian Tracy - Is a Self-Made Millionaire and Author of over eighty books, he reveals his thoughts on goals: "*People with clear written goals accomplish more in a shorter period of time than people without them could ever imagine.*"

Michael Jordan - World Famous Basketball Champion shares his thoughts on the importance of goals: "*I'm a firm believer in goal setting. Step by Step. I can't see any other way of accomplishing things.*"

Albert Einstein - One of the greatest physicists of all time also knew something about the importance of goals: "*If you want to live a happy life, tie it to a goal, not to people or things.*"

LL Cool J - Record Producer, Rapper, and Actor told his followers this: *"Stay focused, go after your dreams, and keep moving toward your goals."*

W. Clement Stone, Insurance Tycoon, Philanthropist, and Author was a big proponent of setting goals, he was always inspiring people, he would tell them: *"No matter how carefully you plan your goals they will never be more than pipe dreams unless you pursue them with gusto."*

Andrew Carnegie, steel magnate and one of the richest men who ever lived, gave this advice on goals: *"If you want to be happy, set a goal that commands your thoughts, liberates your energy and inspires your hopes."*

Success Author and Motivational Speaker Tony Robbins tells his followers: *"Setting goals is the first step in turning the invisible into the visible."*

Pablo Picasso - One of the most famous artists in the world had this to say about goal setting: *"Our goals can only be reached through a vehicle of a plan in which we must fervently believe, and upon which we must vigorously act, there is no other route to success."*

James Cameron - Famous Movie Director, Terminator, Titanic, Etc. Shares his thoughts on goal setting: *"If you set your goals ridiculously high an d it's a failure, you will fail above everyone else's success."*

Muhammad Ali - Heavyweight Boxing Champion Tells the world his secret: *"What keeps me going is goals."*

Earl Nightingale - Known as the Dean of Personal Development said: *"People with goals succeed because they know where they are going. It's as simple as that."*

They all seem to be willing even eager to share with us their knowledge, and I've come to this conclusion. If there is one powerful thing that can move your life to where you want it to be, it is goal setting.

I could continue my search and find many more successful people singing the praises of goal setting for one simple reason. A goal is nothing more than a clear picture of what you want. Knowing what you want is absolutely necessary if you are to reach any objective. Everything in your life, that you have acquired, through your own efforts, was once just a vision. In other words, you had a goal, you took action, you followed through, and it became your reality.

Goal setting speeds things up and helps you achieve more because once you have set a goal, your mind goes to work helping you find ways to reach it. If you can see your goal clearly, and have a strong desire for it, you will be energized to take action to get it, at that point it is almost guaranteed that you will succeed.

As Oprah said, you must stay focused. This is vital, you must keep the goal locked in your mind, or it will evaporate like steam rising after a sun shower. W. Clement Stone also mentioned above said that we should: *"Keep our mind on what we want and off what we don't want."*

May I suggest two ways to do this: One, write your number one goal at odd times during the day, just write one word on a pad, scrap, napkin, or whatever. A single word that represents what you want, this should give you a feeling of pleasure as if you had already achieved it. Writing the goal down, keeps you focused with emotional power, and that keeps your goal alive.

Two, ask yourself this question: "What is the most practical goal step I can take right now?"

You can carry this as a written question, or put it on your PC or cell phone screen, anything that will remind you every day to keep pursuing your goal.

All of the successful people you met in this chapter are just like you; what I'm saying is this: You would not be reading this book if you were not a success seeker. I'm also believing that what they said had a ring of truth for you. Success is not a mystery it's simply setting and reaching your own personal goals. You've achieved success many times, just take a moment to think of all the things you've achieved, it will raise your confidence. When you set a goal it is like setting a GPS direction for your life, now all you have to do is keep going until you reach your destination. Imagine how wonderful it's going to feel when your inducted into this exclusive club of goal setters.

Chapter 42
Will Power

"We must all suffer from one of two pains: The pain of discipline or the pain of regret. The difference is discipline weighs ounces while regret weighs tons."

Jim Rohn

This chapter is not going to be an easy one, but if you hang in and get through it I believe you will understand how discipline and will power can give you the winners edge.

Are you going to live a successful life, a miserable life, or somewhere in between? There is an easy way to determine this. Today you will have many opportunities that will determine how well you will live now and in the future. The opportunities we are talking about are not new to you, you've been accepting or rejecting them all your life. From morning to night, you have been faced with two choices, they are identified by the Jim Rohn quote at the beginning of this chapter. Discipline or Regret, both are painful, but one will lead you to success and the other will lead you to misery. Discipline means you do something you dislike doing because you know it will make your life better. Regret is the awful pain you feel when you put off doing something that needs to be done. Not a day goes by that you don't face, demands, problems, and obligations that need to be met; that's life.

Imagine if a way existed that turned every daily decision into growing strength for the future. Such a way exists, and it's the opportunity of a lifetime, but most people will never consider adopting this way of life. Why? Because to choose discipline over regret is difficult, even though we know the correct choice will lead to a better life. Discipline can make your whole life go more smoothly, and yet there is a good chance you will pass up this opportunity. It is not hard to understand why choosing the better outcome is difficult. It requires developing the rarest ability you can find in any group of people. Will Power! Yes, will power is the ultimate answer for almost every difficulty we face. I know that sounds like an overstatement, but will power is potent, it can burst through the walls of fear, fatigue, and reluctance. Statesman Benjamin Disraeli had this to say: *"Nothing can withstand the power of the human will if it is willing to stake its very existence to the extent of its purpose."* Dreamers have used this power throughout history to fulfill their magnificent wishes, and you too can use it to your advantage. A strong will empowers you to gain your fondest desires.

Developing Will Power

You 've heard the following saying a countless number of times "Where there's a will there's a way" It is a winning perspective, and it continues to be repeated because it's true. How can a person build will power? A person can start by seeing each one of life's daily demands as an opportunity to develop will power. It's a simple choice, and we face it all the time. We must choose correctly between discipline and regret. We are designed to seize advantages, so seeing problems as opportunities gives us an incentive to get into action. Imagine seeing every difficult chore as a chance to develop more will power? Developing will power is a difficult mountain to climb, but if you are up to the challenge the rewards of gaining this power are fantastic.

If a strong will is beneficial, why don't we see people desperately seeking to gain this power? People would rather escape from their everyday pressures; they want life to be a never-ending vacation. Interestingly, the sunny life of leisure they long for can be reached, but only when they go through the door marked discipline. One of our strongest desires is to procrastinate, but when we go through that door we wind up in the land of regret. All stressed out, we cannot bring ourselves to do the things that need doing. This lack of diligence piles regret upon regret, and we miss out on having the tranquil life we desire.

Can we identify what's behind this disruptive behavior? Yes, it's false fear. Anxiety from irrational fear causes us to put off doing what is necessary to make our life easier. Nature designed us to be fearful, to make sure we look before we leap, so we can survive in a hostile world. Nature's plan has worked well for roughly 6 million years from the time of early human development. Despite all the threats from famine, floods, and wars we're still here. Today, human intelligence has made progress, and we live in a more civilized and technologically advanced world. Consequently, there is less danger, and we should be able to enjoy the safety and advances humankind has won. Sadly, we take no comfort in our increased security because our biological make-up has not changed. Most fear today is unwarranted but tell that to your emotions. Too often we are victims of our own absurd fear. Smothered by a false fear we become dormant and we miss out on the joy of living. It is still wise to be cautious, but not to see fear everywhere. No one stops to think, is this real or irrational fear? Our natural feelings are designed to protect us, but they can produce an unwarranted sense of caution that causes us to procrastinate. Dread causes people to avoid doing a simple task, and they put it off for another day. This lack of will causes burdens to pile up and soon we are overwhelmed, a victim of our own inaction. This brings on the horrendous feeling of regret, and we know that we did not take the action that would have brought relief. Looking back it seemed we had an easy choice before us, but fear shut us down, and like a bear in winter we hibernated. Too bad Mark Twain was not there to advise us, he said: *"Do the thing you fear and the death of fear is certain."*

The choice is yours, have the discipline to do the right thing or choose the easy way out and feel the pain of regret. We all know from experience that it takes will power to make the right choice. If you develop will power, it becomes easy to make good decisions. Armed with a strong will, everything in your life will change for the better. When you face down fear you feel more alive, and you accomplish more.

Starting now, every time you face one of life's challenges you can see it as an opportunity, to develop will power. This will be the trigger for you to challenge yourself to do the difficult thing. Imagine for a moment, how many good opportunities will appear every day in your life. The more opportunities the better, this will be your new attitude.

Every good choice between discipline and regret not only increases your will power, but it leads to successful living. Today challenge yourself to make just one difficult decision in your favor. One at a time these brave decisions will mount up moving aggravating things out of your way, and soon you'll look out on your horizon and see nothing but clear sailing. More importantly you'll be building will power. With every good decision, you'll feel pride, not regret. If you're fearful and waiting for just the right mood, you'll wait forever. Just take some little action to get started and it's likely that inspiration will come out of the blue. What were we avoiding, now it seems so easy? When you're frozen with fear you're immobilized, you feel helpless. With will power you burst out from the deep freeze and live the warm happy life you've hoped for. You'll go from a life where nothing was happening, to reaching dreams you thought were unreachable. You can do it! Jump at every chance to develop your will power, plunge right in and tackle the problem before you. Challenge yourself to do just one of the difficult things haunting you. When you dare yourself, you'll find it pumps up your courage, and it gives you a sense of urgency. Insurance tycoon W. Clement Stone put it this way: *"Thinking won't overcome fear, but action will."* That's the trick; all the doers in this world know this: Action! Action! Action! Get into action now, and you'll feel exhilaration as you escape from false fear. A strong will puts you in control of your life, your time, and your finances. Develop will power and you will create an unrelenting will to win. Armed with will power you become an irresistible force. Now your only need is an admirable undertaking. We started this chapter with a quote by Jim Rohn and he has this suggestion for you: "*Whoever renders service to many puts himself in line for greatness – great wealth, great return, great satisfaction, great reputation, and great joy.*"

Chapter 43
Live In Paradise

By staying reward minded you can be living in your own paradise. With that statement, I'm sure I'm putting my credibility on the line. Let me clarify, and then I think you'll agree with me. If you are looking forward to a good thing happening in your life, you know this type of thinking puts you in a good mood.

Most of what is happening to you and me is all in our thoughts about the future, we're thinking about the next thing we're going to do, or experience. If we expect a positive happening, we feel good, if not we may feel dread or some other negative feeling. The amount of time we devote to imagining how our life will be, is likely equal or greater than the actual time we spend living it. Since we are spending so much time projecting our future, we can start to have a much happier life by entertaining a more enjoyable outlook. With a bright expectation, we tend to luxuriate in this wonder we call life. This positive attitude makes us more inclined to take the bold actions needed to improve our real life.

Gratitude is another mood lifter, if we choose to be grateful for what we have it generates a good feeling within us. Your life may not be perfect at this moment in time, but with gratitude and high expectations you'll tend to move towards the life you imagine. The quality of our life is essentially determined by the thoughts we think. Encouraging thoughts fire up our emotions, and they can give us the courage we need to solve problems facing us. We will take more of an active role in our life situation and not just let whatever will be, will be. We never have total control, and we all rely on others to help us. The human race can only survive with all of us serving one another. Energy that leads to action is the only way we can make our real life better.

The following insight may be repetitious, but it's worth repeating. Once a person discovers that they have the power to choose their thoughts, an equally powerful revelation is illuminated. It becomes clear that our thoughts will also have a strong influence on our state of happiness or misery. You've heard the old saying "Four walls do not a prison make." Even if you were unfortunate enough to be in prison you could still find moments of happiness by slipping into a daydream of a happier time and place. Once you learn how to think this way you can always drift away to a place where life is perfect. You can live in paradise.

Many people refer to this as Pollyannaish thinking, but that would miss the real point of this chapter. No matter what your current life situation, your thoughts are the dominate force that will shape your life and the way you live. Superstar baseball player Wade Boggs put it this way. *"A positive attitude causes a chain reaction of positive thoughts, events and outcomes. It is a catalyst and it sparks extraordinary results."*

Observe that most of the winners in life tend to keep on winning, that's because they've formed habits that lead to success. The most important success habit is thinking about what we want. It's not all that easy to hold fast to an empowering thought because life's demands are always competing for our attention. Passionately wanting something is the impetus that leads to action. Persistent action is essential for success, but it does not happen without persistent thinking. The winners in life are simply dwelling on what they want. High expectations generate joyful feelings, and they can't wait to experience the real thing. (Often in life the excitement of the chase is more satisfying than the actual victory) Like a greyhound chasing the rabbit, winners are addicted to the euphoria of the chase. Knowing what they want gives winners a leg up on people whose desires just flicker on and off at random.

Would you like to experience for yourself what having a fixed aim in life can do for you? Why not try it, not only will it make you happy, but it gives you the power to make it happen. Everything you want gravitates towards you when you steadily dwell on a positive desire. It's not instantaneous, but it is inevitable given enough time. Your next question might be how? It's a learning experience so let's go through this step by step. As we've discussed, we're not always living in the moment but we're viewing our past or future life. How can these positive fantasies work to make your life more perfect? You hold a vision of the future, seeing your life the way you would like it to be. Choose the thoughts you are thinking, just as carefully as you would choose a movie you want to see in a theater or on Netflix. You certainly don't want to sit through a boring movie or a dreary life. When you're watching a movie, you suspend disbelief, and you pretend it's really happening. Your emotions are not logical, and they don't know the difference between real life, and what is happening on your mental screen. That's why people cry at the movies. When your emotions are strong enough, the intensity of your desire, naturally overcomes fear and reluctance. Your thinking is now fused with determination, you're talking to yourself with statements such as "I can handle this, I know what to do, this is really not all that difficult." Action is the giant leap forward, once in motion your closing in on success. The odds are in your favor and there is an excellent chance you will awaken one day living the wonderful future you've only imagined.

Chapter 44
Planting Seeds

"Whatever we plant in our subconscious mind and nourish with repetition and emotion will one day become a reality."

Earl Nightingale

Once an emotion charged idea has firmly taken root in your mind, it will seek to replicate itself in a physical way. The energy that makes this happen is an eager state of mental anticipation. This mental state is what military commander Ferdinand Foch was talking about when he said *"The most powerful weapon on earth is the human soul on fire."*
Take a moment to think of something that you really yearn for, something that makes you happy. Dwell on it until it becomes a sizzling desire. If you can hold this thought, it will act just like a seed. It will sprout up and start to take root in your mind. Writing this desire down will also nurture a growing want within you as the tiny seed starts to sprout. If you can think of some simple action that helps you get closer to making this idea real in your life, the roots will grow deeper and take a more permanent hold. A sharp focus on this desire will provide the sunshine needed to help sustain the plants growth. Feeling excitement when you think that it just might be possible, is like watering and fertilizing with

desire, this keeps the plant alive. At this stage you start to realize that the little seedling you planted has the potential to bloom into reality. Now your excitement is building because the thought you planted has blossomed into a fervent desire, and it is growing in the rich soil of belief and expectancy. With all the constant attention you've given to this plant your craving has grown into full bloom. It's something that you must have because you're convinced it will make you deliriously happy.

Now it's harvest time. You are ready do what you know you must do. Push through fear, give no thought to doubt, and most important take action. It's likely you will hit obstacles, but don't even think about stopping, you can find a way to get by them. With persistence you will be joyfully living your dream. Now take some time to relax and enjoy your success until you're ready to plant another seed.

Chapter 45
Happy Ending

"Life's like a movie, write your own ending.
Keep believing, keep pretending."

Jim Henson

You have reached the last chapter in this book, proving that you have made Unrelenting Little Efforts. That fact alone means that it's very likely you are a doer, a member of that elite group who can get things done. I hope this book has helped you to discover ways to kick your motivation into high gear, because when you're psyched up you multiply your chances of being successful. The promise of this book is that you can get what you want. The chapter on Goal Setting gives you the key to that door. It's a simple formula write the goal down, make it a high priority in your life, and get into action. Once you are in action, metaphorically speaking you will be obeying Newton's 1st law of motion. "A body in motion tends to stay in motion unless acted on by an outside force." Take at least one baby step, because all you need are a series of Unrelenting Little Efforts to arrive at your destination. Finally make a commitment to yourself that you will persist; that you will never give up. Once you're totally absorbed in your single-minded pursuit, you will achieve your dreams, you have no alternative but to become successful.

TABLE OF CONTENTS

Lightning Source UK Ltd.
Milton Keynes UK
UKHW012015171022
410614UK00006B/1233

9 791220 122856